First published in Australia in 2006 by
New Holland Publishers (Australia) Pty Ltd
Sydney • Auckland • London • Cape Town

14 Aquatic Drive Frenchs Forest NSW 2086 Australia
218 Lake Road Northcote Auckland New Zealand
86 Edgware Road London W2 2EA United Kingdom
80 McKenzie Street Cape Town 8001 South Africa

Copyright © 2006 in text: Janelle McCulloch
Copyright © 2006 in photographs: Janelle McCulloch
Copyright © 2006 New Holland Publishers (Australia) Pty Ltd

All rights reserved. No part of this publication may be reproduced, stored in a retrieval system or transmitted, in any form or by any means, electronic, mechanical, photocopying, recording or otherwise, without the prior written permission of the publishers and copyright holders.

10 9 8 7 6 5 4 3 2 1
National Library of Australia Cataloguing-in-Publication Data:

McCulloch, Janelle.
      Country estates.

      ISBN 1 74110 466 1.

      1. Country homes - Australia - Pictorial works. I. Title.

      728.80994

Publisher: Fiona Schultz
Managing Editor: Martin Ford
Designers: Janelle McCulloch, Leigh Nankervis
Production Manager: Linda Bottari
Printer: C&C Offset Printing Company, China

Front Cover photo: Larundel
Back Cover photo: Kennerton Green

It is only in the country that we can get to know a person or a book...

       Cyril Connolly, 1945

Country Estates

of Australia

Cottages, Farmhouses, Manors and Mansions

Written and photographed by

Janelle McCulloch

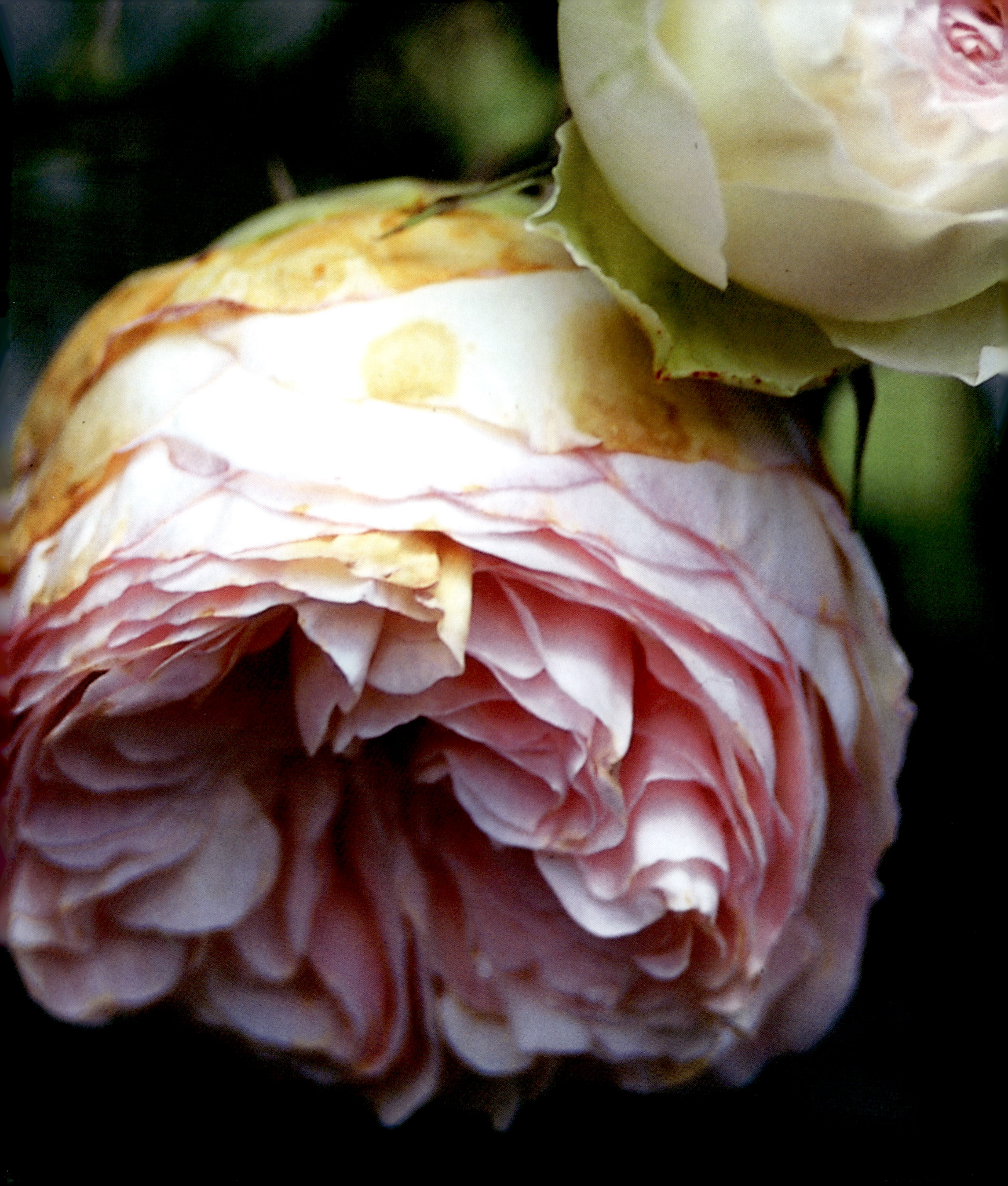

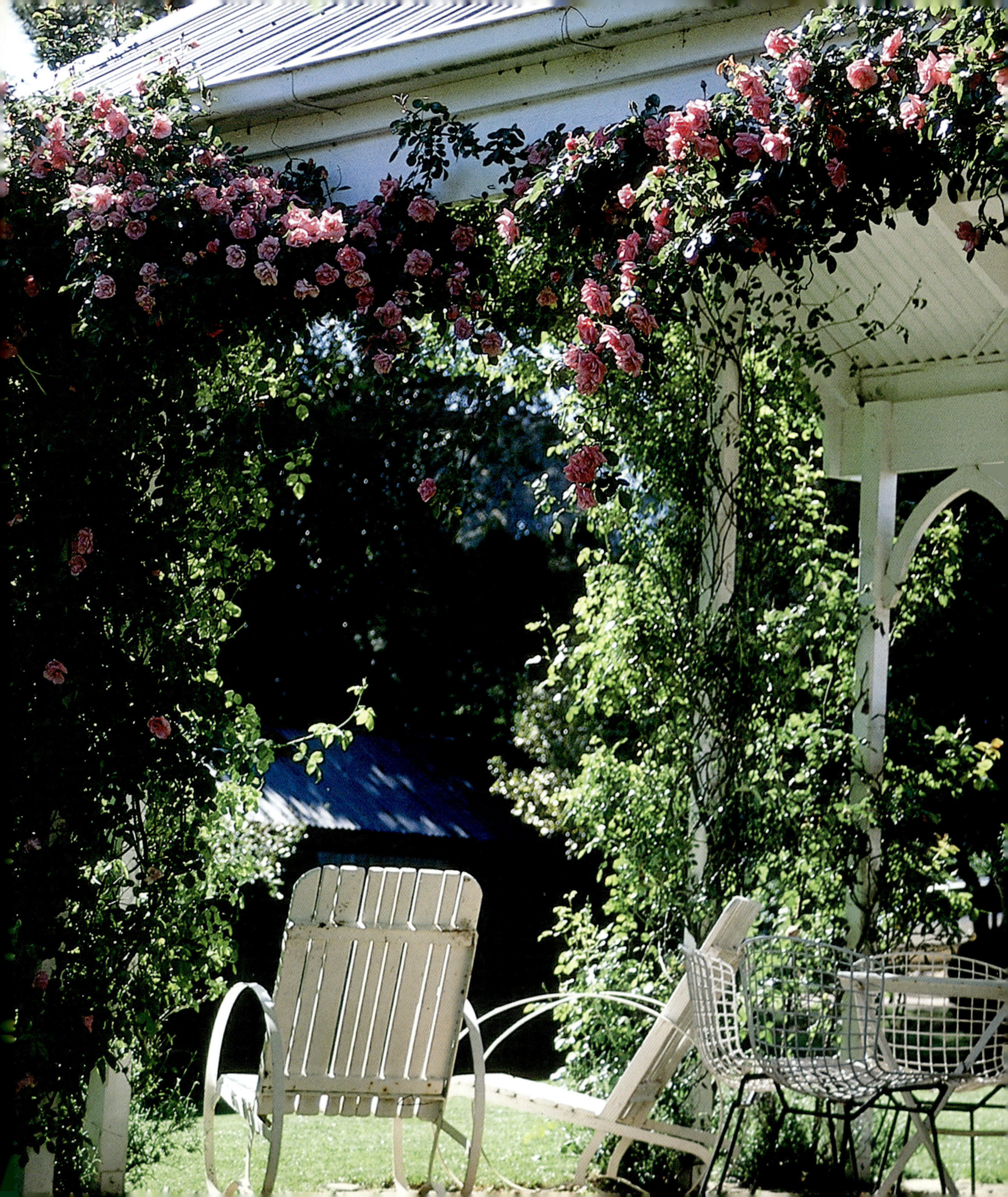

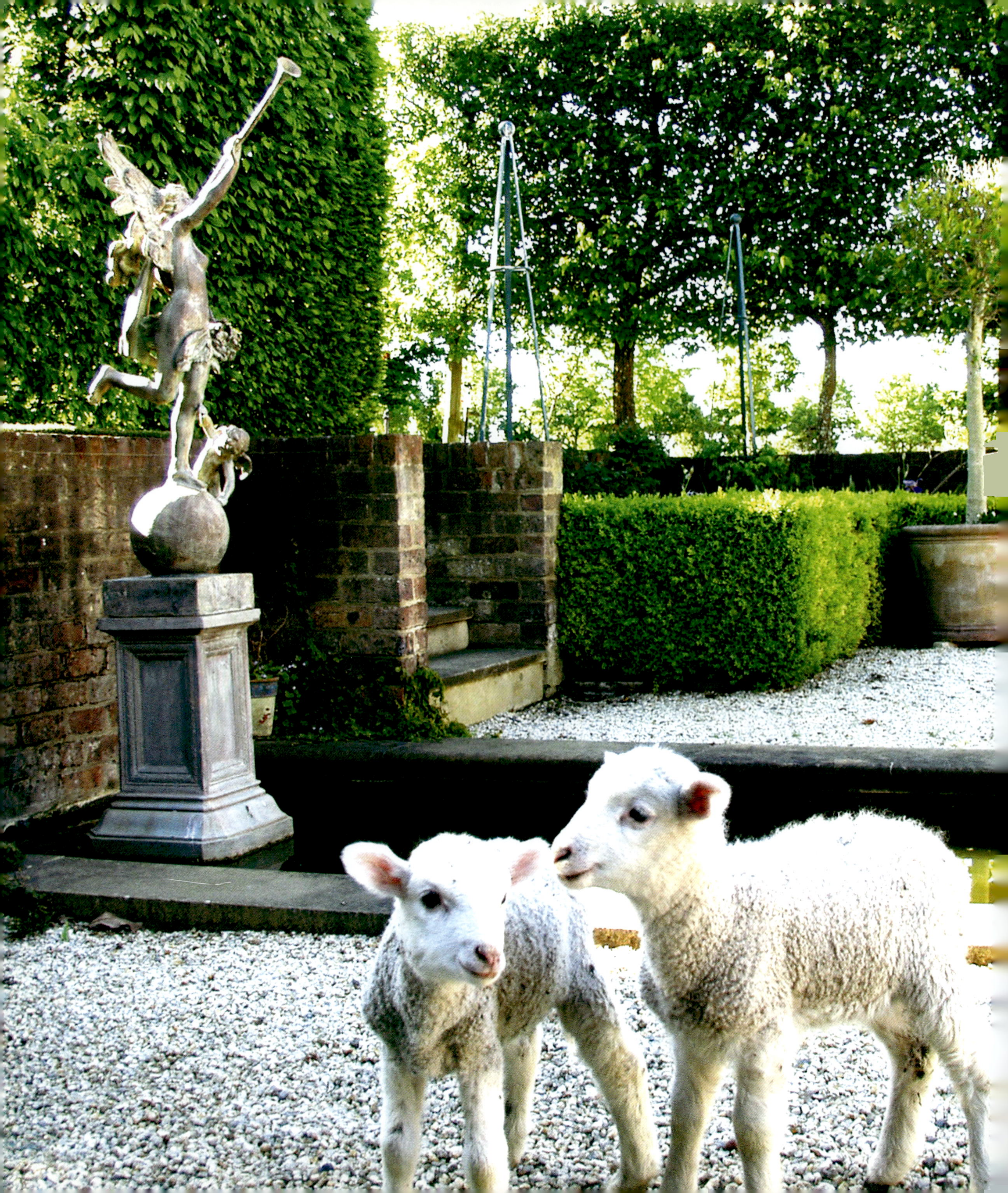

Contents

Cottages & Farmhouses

THE DESIGNER'S FARMHOUSE:
Fern Vale Farm — 16

THE LAVENDER FARM:
Lavandula — 30

THE COUNTRY GARDEN:
Kennerton Green — 42

THE DESIGNER'S GARDEN:
St Ambrose Farm — 50

THE CREATIVE HIDEAWAY:
Mulabinba — 64

THE VINEYARD:
Spray Farm — 76

Great Country Houses

THE GREAT ESTATE:
Larundel — 88

THE GOUMET HAUNT:
Yandina Station — 110

THE CATTLE STATION:
Burrawang West Station — 124

THE MOUNTAIN HIDEAWAY:
Duneira — 132

THE HILLTOP RETREAT:
Cameron Lodge — 138

Grand Mansions

THE ARCADIAN IDYLL:
Dalvui — 150

THE SCOTTISH-INSPIRED COUNTRY SEAT:
Ercildoune — 160

THE ROMANTIC COUNTRY HOUSE:
Hopewood — 176

THE FAMILY HOME:
Belltrees — 184

Introduction

Country estates have always held a fascination for people. They represent the epitome of glamour and grandeur; a place where people seem to live far more interesting lives than we do.

Much of this fascination, it could be argued, stems from centuries ago, when such properties were considered the 'power houses' of aristocratic society, with their grand façades, great gardens, vast agricultural estates and extravagant parties. Their owners, who were usually already members of the aristocracy or landed gentry, often used these lofty properties to leverage themselves to an even higher social status, building extensive wings, commissioning magnificent gardens and hosting ever more lavish balls in order to reflect their wealth, power, influence and of course their ambitious aspirations. So serious were they about their country houses that owners regularly embarked on excursions around England to snatch architectural inspiration from others' estates – all on the pretence of a 'social visit', of course.

Author Malcolm Kendall in his book *The Great Good Place* discusses this very subject and says there was always a clear distinction between the *villa rustica* (the working farm) and the *villa urbana* (the country house). The latter, he says, was firmly the domain of the gentleman, who furnished it in opulent fashion with priceless pieces picked up from far-flung destinations visited on the Grand Tour.

Not surprisingly, the demanding costs associated with maintaining such a house were always an issue for owners, no matter how wealthy they were. Writer Meghan Hayward, in her *Country House* essay, revealed that an 1826 visitor to England once remarked that 'it requires considerable fortune to keep up a country estate, for custom demands a handsomely fitted-up house with elegant furniture, servants in liveries, a profusion of dishes and foreign wines'. Considering most of the larger country house encompassed at least 25 – sometimes even 50 – rooms and covered at least 8,000 square feet of floor space, including service rooms, it's easy to understand how the food, wine, staff, entertaining and maintenance bills could blow out to stately proportions.

Several centuries later, the political powers of the land-owning class have declined, and so have the properties they once owned. Today, the once great country house has, like a formerly formidable duchess, sadly diminished in size and stature. Too expensive to maintain without a legion of servants bustling about the labyrinthine halls, these homes have slowly dwindled in number until now there are only a select few left. Those that are left in private hands in Australia survive on vastly reduced estates, and are often propped up by funds from classical concerts, operas or open days.

But while the fortunes and estates of country houses have declined, the idyllic life they represent hasn't dissipated. In fact – and with a small amount of irony – the fascination for them has only increased as the threat of their demise grows ever more real.

Such is the interest in them that urban professionals are now venturing out to rural areas to find their own Arcadian idyll; a place where they can go to escape the population and pace of the modern metropolis. While many try to relive the past and all its grandeur and glory by restoring a once magnificent estate, others are content to invest in a smaller abode, knowing that their modest cottage epitomises the same country house values.

This book is a tribute to these country properties, whether great or small; to their history, dignity, and of course their romance, as they continue to inspire us, even through modern times. From quaint country houses to grand country manors, sophisticated gentlemen's retreats and sweeping pastoral stations, *Country Estates* offers an extraordinary insight into the richness and spirit of these places, and provides an intimate sense of what it means to inhabit one. As Jane Austen once said, 'if only we could all live in such a place'.

Janelle McCulloch

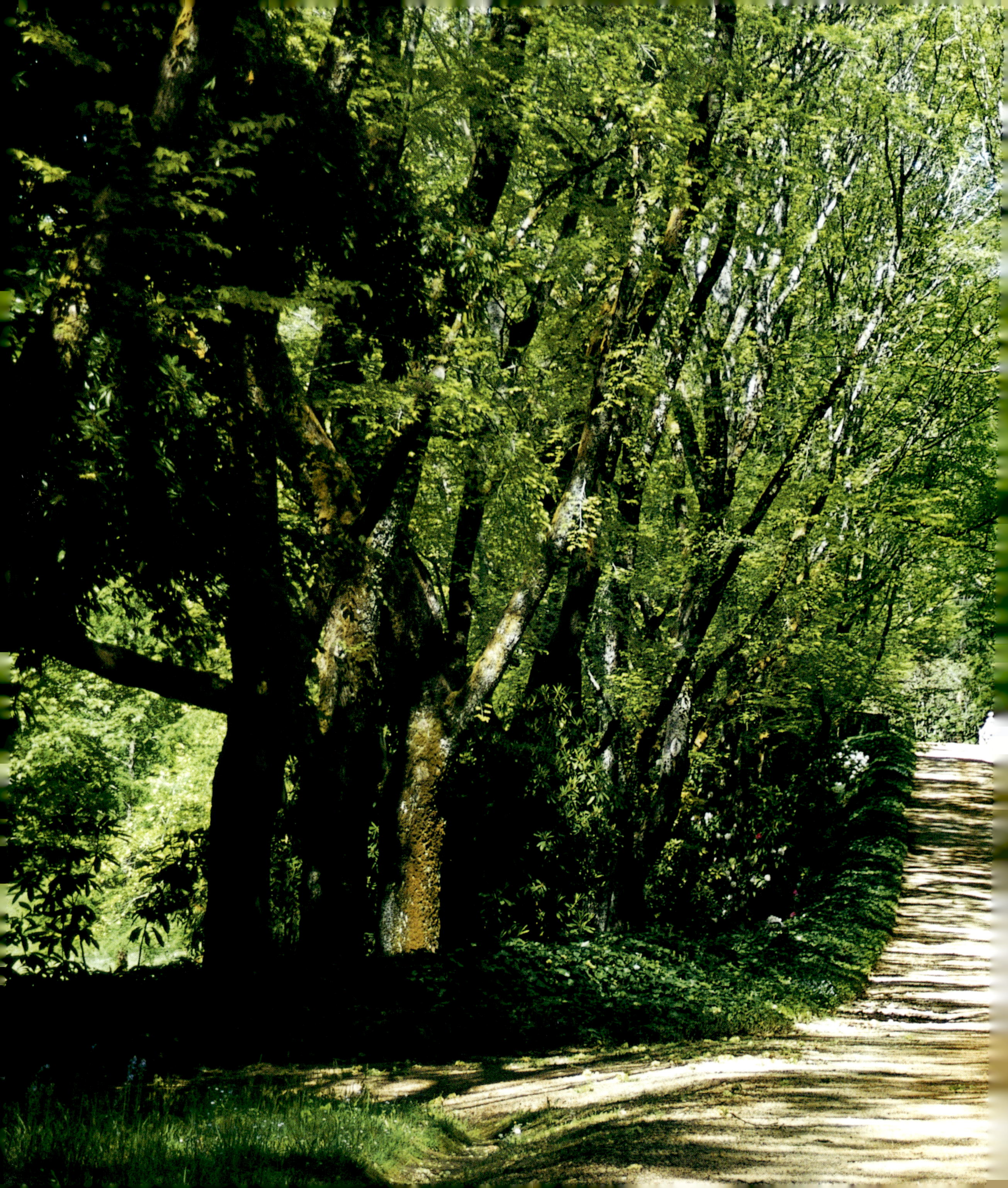

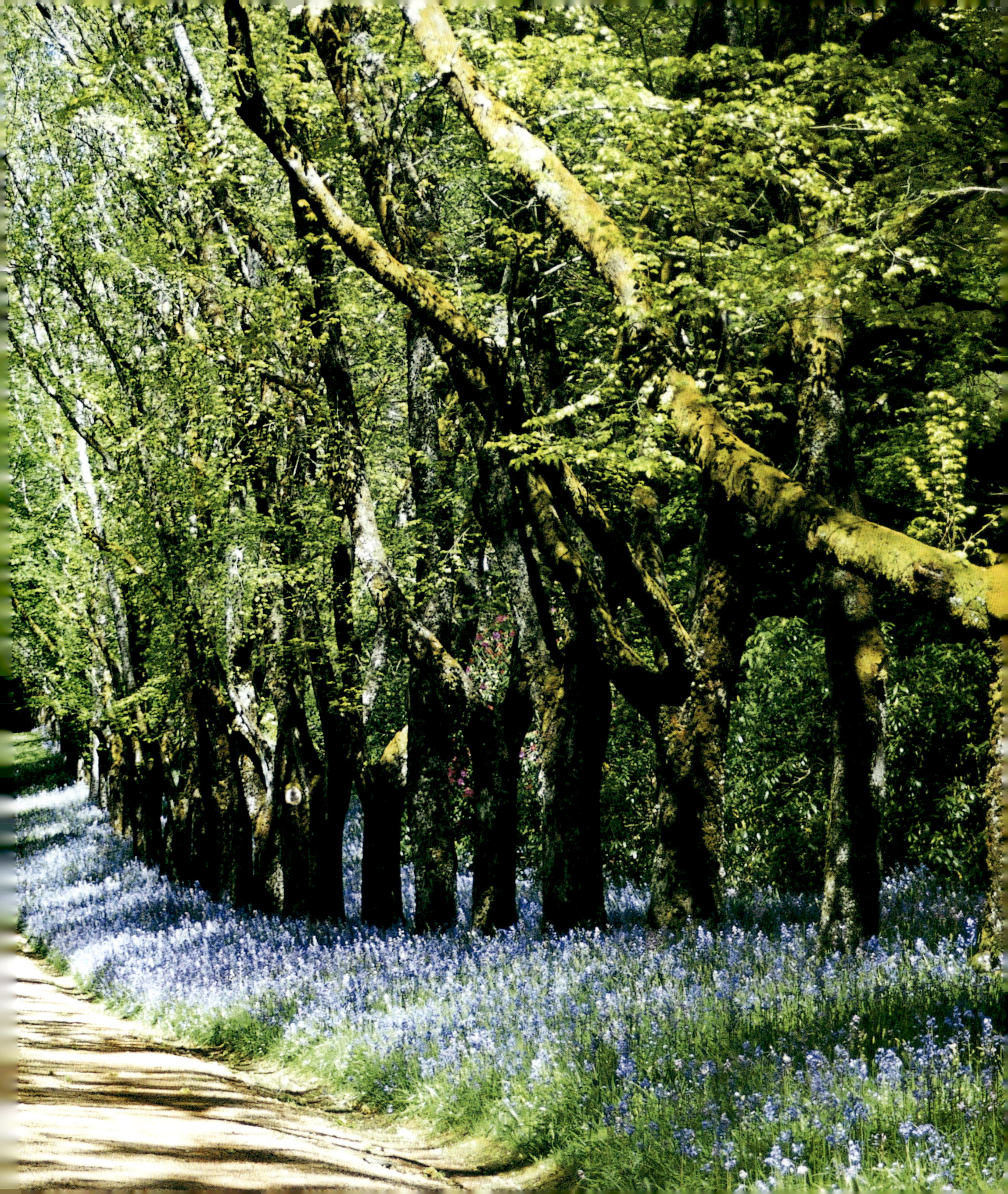

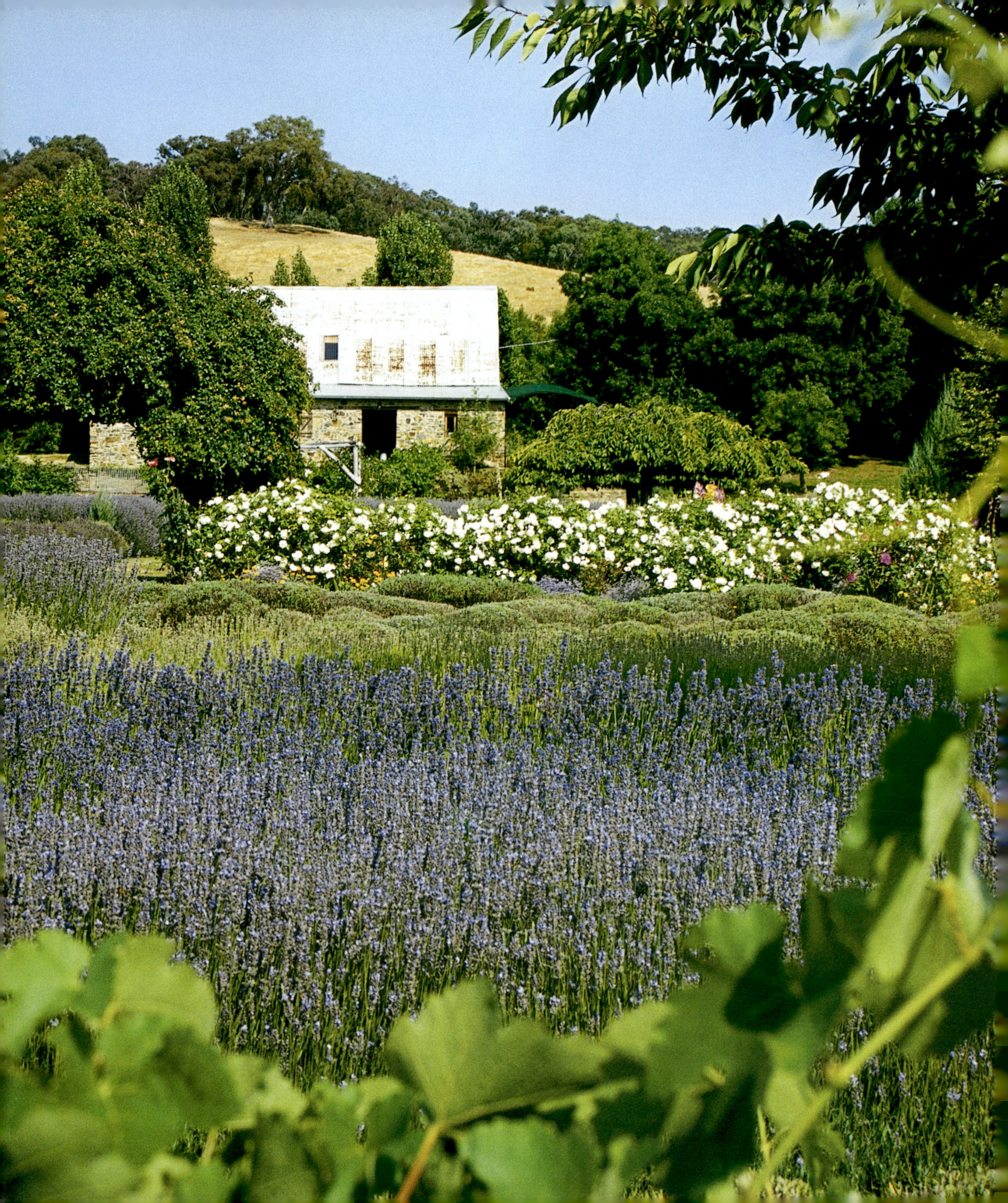

Cottages & Farmhouses

Fern Vale Farm

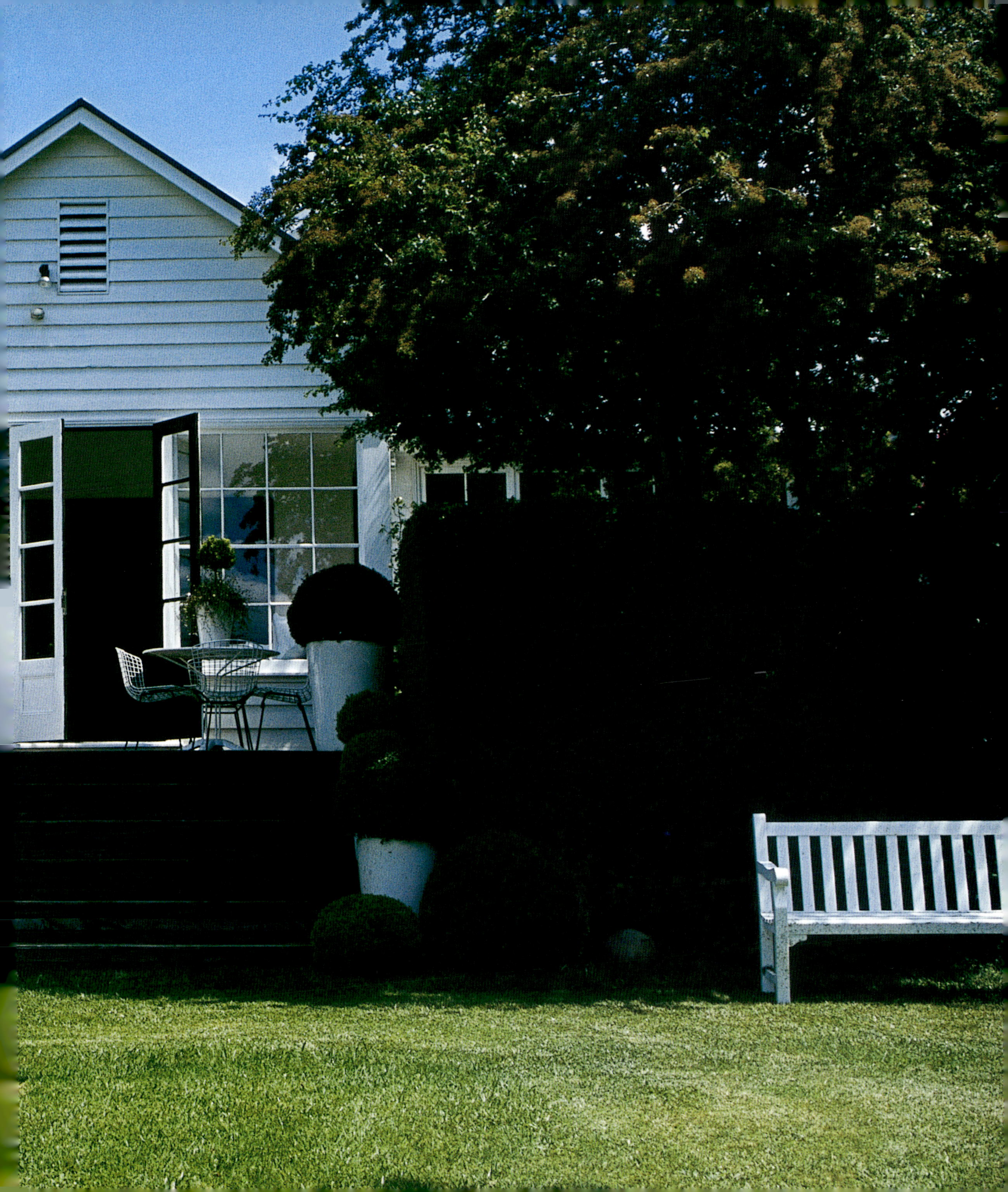

Redesigning a century-old country house obviously involves different parameters than a modern house in town but owner and interior designer Jane Charlwood has conquered any problems here with quiet élan. Bedrooms have been opened up with litres of white paint, bathrooms have been skillfully carved out of corners, and the principal rooms have been reconfigured so that they now flow together to create sheer interior poetry.

It is rare to find a country house filled with modern pieces. Normally an Arne Jacobsen chair or a Philippe Starck stool would look too, well, Starck – pun intended – in a place fit for linen, gingham and distressed wood. But at Jane Charlwood's house, on the quiet side of Mount Macedon, modern has not only found a very comfortable home with its casual country cousin, it has elevated the latter to a cool new level of style.

Tucked away down the end of a holly lane, like some fabulous fairytale-style hideaway, Fern Vale Farm is one part magic, one part minimalist chic. When Charlwood, a Melbourne-based interior designer, first purchased the property, however, it was dark, cluttered and recovering from a period as a bed and breakfast. The house, which is over a century old, was worn out, and looked it. Charlwood's father suggested she pull the lot down.

But, like so many who fall in love with a country house, Charlwood wanted to save it: she felt the house still had soul, and a spirit. So the 'rabbit warren of rooms', as she calls them, were opened up and reconfigured into more liveable areas suited to two city professionals – and the friends and family who would inevitably follow.

Five bedrooms and three swish new ensuites were carved out of the former bed and breakfast rooms, while a sunny kitchen, a beautiful long dining space, a cosy library, a country office, a fabulous living room and a spectacular sunroom flowing out to a deck and then down to a playing field-sized lawn hemmed by hedges and mowed to perfection for summer soirées were created out of the rest of the property.

Of course, the facelift took a little more than some clever architecture. The harmonious balance of big open rooms and small intimate ones was achieved by hundreds of litres of white paint, which Charlwood used to 'open' up the formerly cramped Bed and Breakfast. Window frames, walls, even floorboards were all finished in a chalky eggshell white that has transformed the house into a gallery-like space fit for the sleek vignettes that have since filled it. Some of the timber was too beautiful to whitewash and so Charlwood simply updated those parts with a rich, glossy chocolate finish, which has made the house a little like architectural confectionery: completely and utterly irresistible.

FERN VALE FARM

With a style that could only be describe as 'modern elegance', Fern Vale Farm is the Audrey Hepburn of country houses: understated in its chic simplicity but also infused with delightful splashes of wit and whimsy. The interior is pure glamour but it is the garden, with its shady nooks and rose-scented crannies, that truly makes this place. There is an enchanting space for every kind of soirée (and Jane Charlwood, a lively hostess, has used them all. Polished to a sophisticated finish, the house has now achieved an apotheosis its original owner may never have imagined.

COUNTRY ESTATES

A TYPICAL WEEKEND AT FERN VALE FARM

SATURDAY: Drive up from Melbourne. Stock up on fine wine and great recipes and bring enough food to feed the troopsof friends and family that will inevitably follow. Check the guestlist for incoming arrivals. Set the deckchairs and cushions out in the shade and reposition the various garden chairs underneath the trees, depending on where lunch will be served. Then check on Archie and the other animals and go for a wander around the garden to see what's grown (or needs to be trimmed).
Decide on a menu for lunch.

SUNDAY: Get up early and go for a walk up to Camel's Hump. Return and set up one of the outside tables for a long, languorous brunch. Fill some vases with flowers, set a pitcher of water in the fridge to chill and pour a big glass of wine. Arrange an enormous table of food under an outside tree and tell the guests to feel at home.

Country houses have always been as much about entertaining as animal husbandry. Indeed, a century ago, the focus was firmly on the conspicuously consumptive. Activities were frivolous, parties large and guests many. It was a long, languorous, lived-to-the-full life of luncheons, hunts, tennis parties, afternoon teas and dressing for dinner. While not quite replicating the formal feel of those early country house parties, Jane Charlwood nonetheless loves nothing more than a long weekend with friends, and for her entertaining efforts has come to be known as one of the best hosts around.

ROOM(S) WITH A VIEW

Once upon a great estate, country houses were built to reflect the amount of land they rested upon. So if there were swathes of paddocks and views to chink a glass of Chateau Lafitte to, you built a stonking mansion with all the literal bells and whistles. If the farm was slightly smaller, you built a more modest abode. And if you started off rich and then lost your wealth, either through a bad poker hand, bad farm management, a bad marriage or death and the inevitable taxes, you – or your family – sold off the land, kept the house and stared through the windows at someone's else's views. Georgian architecture, in particular, was very big on views, so if you lost yours during the Georgian times it was truly a bad thing.

The grandest country houses were positioned according to this all-important vista, both so that the country squire could stare out at his domain, whisky in hand and hound dog at his feet, and the visiting guests could stare, suitably impressed, right back at him as they trundled up the driveway.

Hills were always good for this. Even today, if you're looking for a country property and you find that you're lost, stop the car and look for the nearest hill. There will inevitably be a country house sitting on top of it.

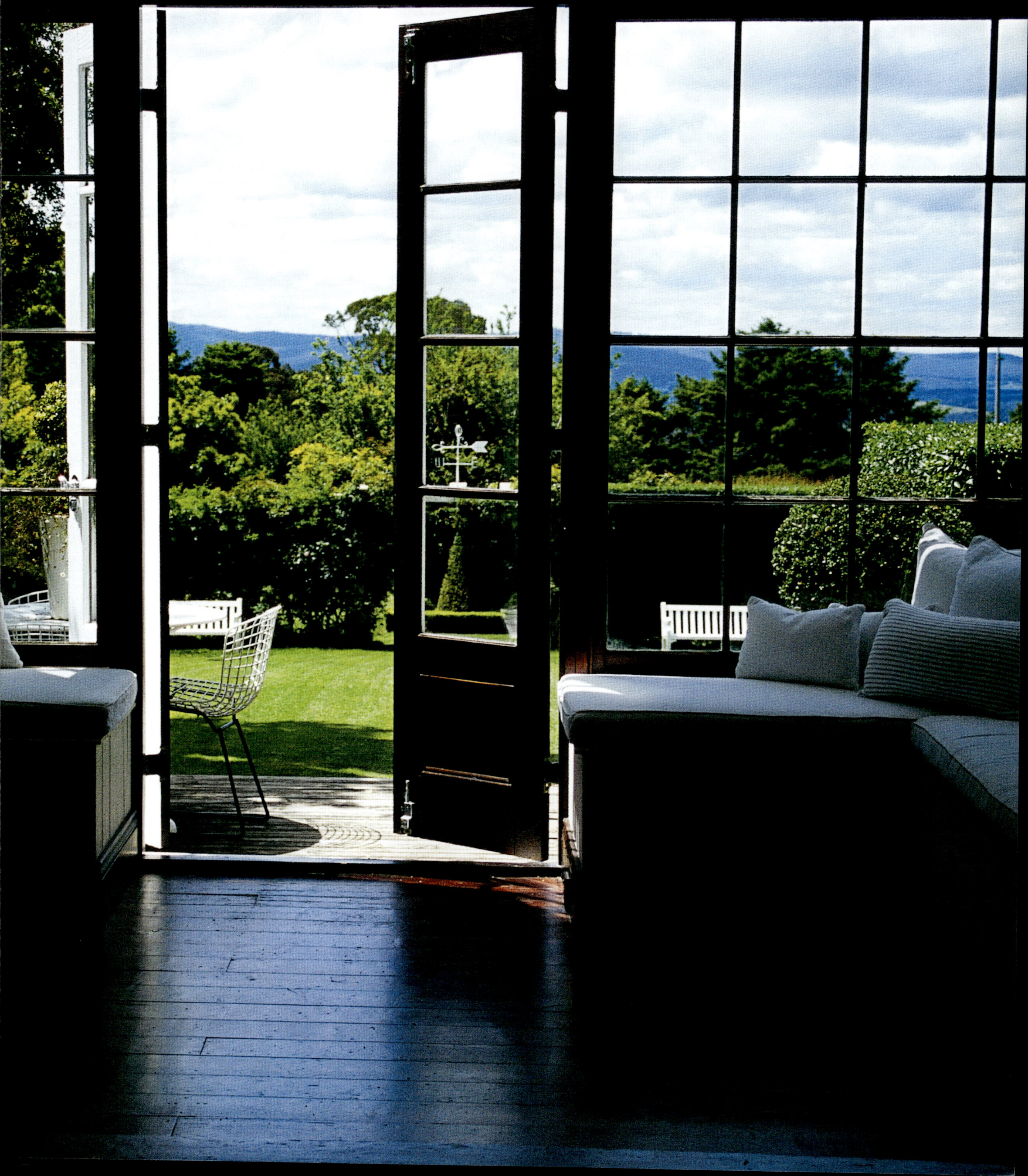

Passionate about design, Jane Charlwood infuses humour and style into everything she does. In the kitchen and library, lemons, plucked fresh from the garden, are placed on sand in a shallow wooden crate – a sort of zen-meets-Mother Nature creation. In the master bedroom, a pared-down fireplace is made into an art piece with the aid of a few carefully placed vintage pieces. And in the glorious dining room, sculpture comes to life in front of a modern painting thanks to an enormous tree branch positioned casually beside two Italian lamps and a tin bucket. Delightful, discerning, and deliriously witty.

COUNTRY ESTATES

ROAST VEGETABLE FRITTATA

INGREDIENTS

leftover roast vegetables (best veggies are sweet potato or pumpkin, baby potatoes, zucchini and onions)
6 eggs
1 cup of cream
1/2 cup parmesan cheese, grated
basil and black pepper

Toss the leftover roast vegetables in a frypan to warm. (If using fresh vegetables, sprinkle with salt and oil and roast as normal in oven until golden brown). Whip the eggs, cream, pepper and basil together and pour into the pan on top of vegetables. Cook over low heat until top is firm. Cut into rough squares and serve with salad.

FERN VALE FARM

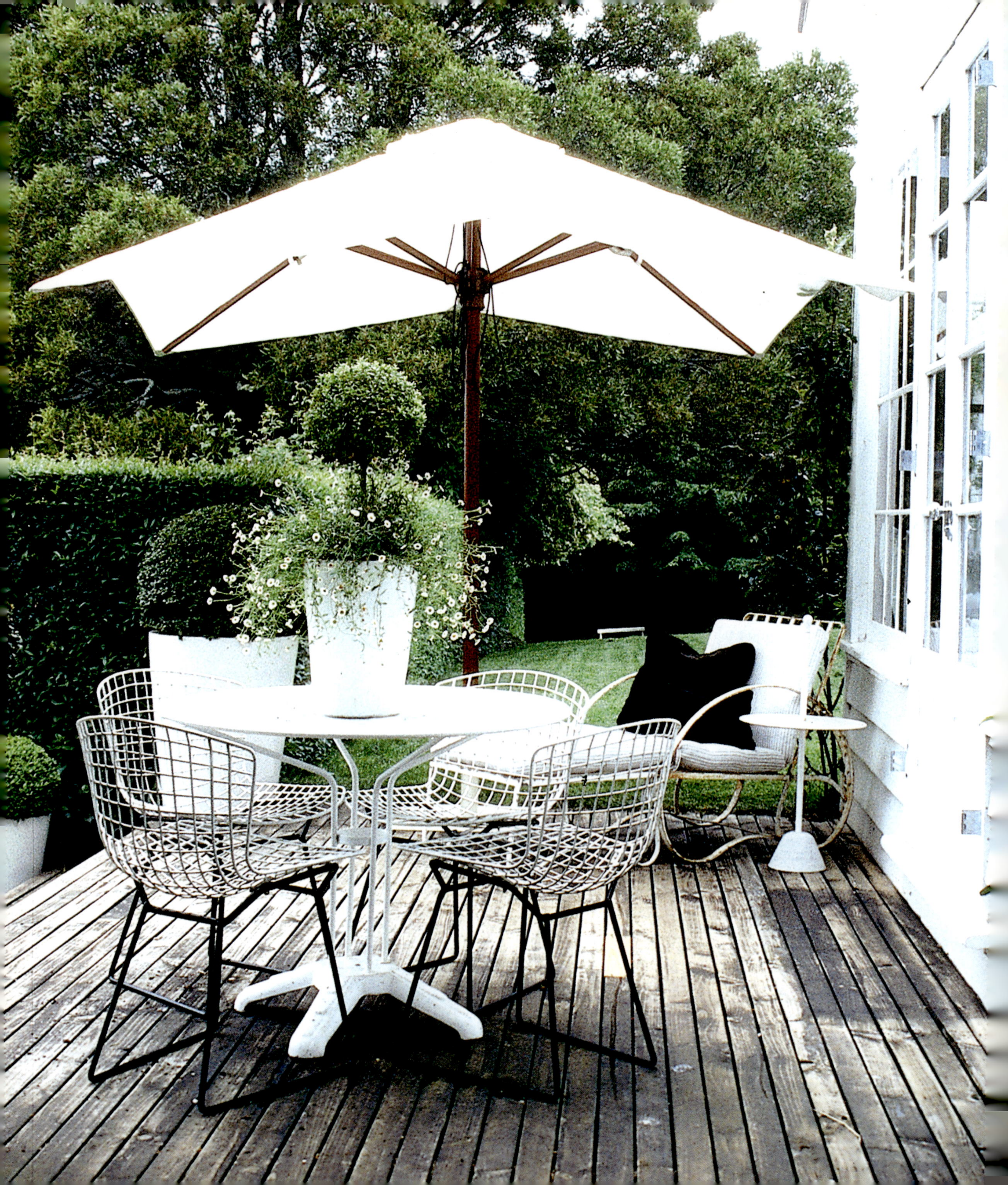

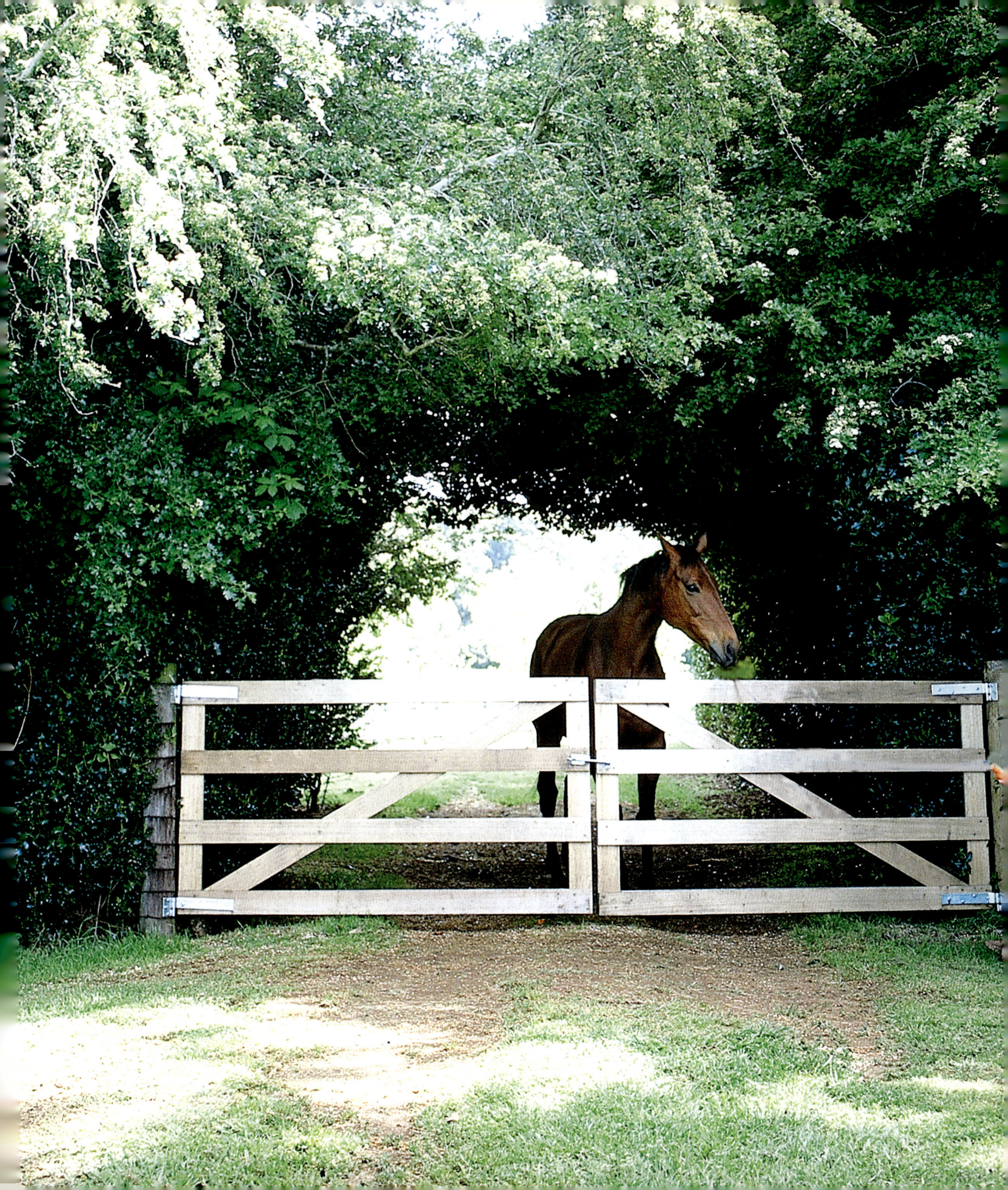

As you would expect at the home of an interior designer, the attention to detail at Fern Vale Farm is extraordinary. In fact, the house and garden are full of glamour in spades, if you'll forgive the pun. The predominant palette is black and white, and even the topiary pots are painted in sophisticated monochrome tones. The deck chairs and chaise lounges, meanwhile, are all accessorised with licorice-coloured cushions – laid-back glamour indeed.

COUNTRY ESTATES

FERN VALE FARM

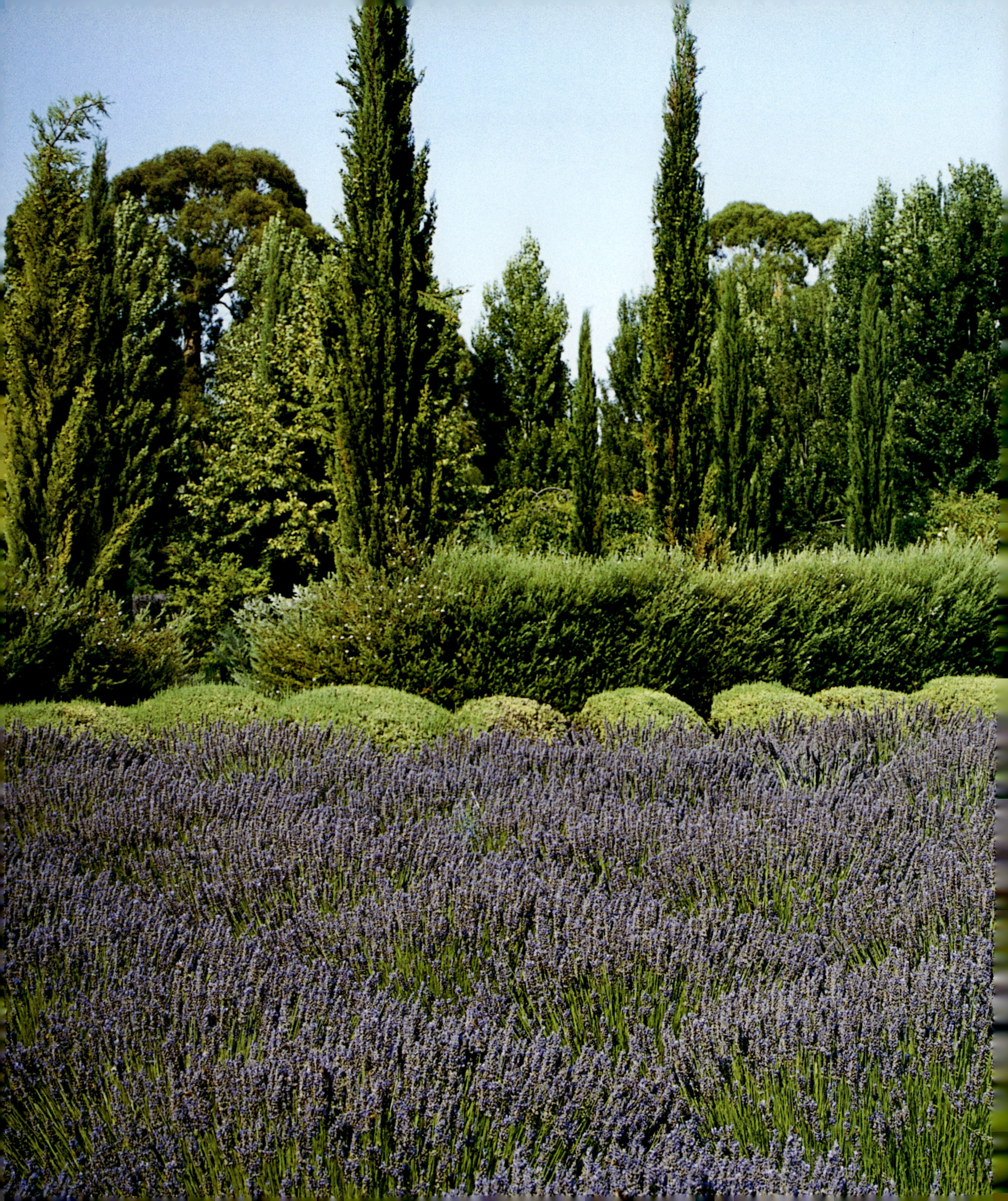

Lavandula

Field of dreams (previous page): the first of the season's new lavender emerges under the protection of a row of poplars. Spanish lavender is in flower from late October while the English lavender is in full bloom from Christmas, when the fields are patterned in white, pink, mauve and deep purple lavenders. During January the flower stems are hand harvested using a sickle, and bunched for sale.

No one knows who originally uttered the words 'as Rosemary is to the spirit, so Lavender is to the soul', but whoever it was, they could well have been referring to Lavandula, one of Australia's most romantic, most entrancing country estates.

Designed by Carol White, a petite Parisian-style businesswoman with a penchant for all things French – and Italian for that matter – this sublime slice of countryside fuses European sensibilities with Australian topography to create an intimate space of truly extraordinary aesthetics.

Entered via a causeway bridge (there is also a pretty suspension footbridge for when the terrain floods) and a poplar-lined driveway, the property opens out to chic collection of perfectly symmetrical lavender 'rooms' and a cluster of thoroughly romantic farmhouse buildings surrounded by olive groves, vineyards and Tuscan-style blue-green hills that roll away into the hazy distance. Carol White's own residence is tucked away here also; an exquisite putty-coloured stone cottage with a shady verandah fronting a cobbled courtyard that looks like it fell lock, stock and wooden door out of a children's storybook.

Built during the 1850s gold rush by the Italian-speaking Swiss immigrants the Tinetti family, who owned and worked the area for 150 years, the stone cottages had been empty for almost 30 years when Carol White stumbled across them. She took possession of the 'rustica' in 1987, and the property required many years of restoration before it began to look like the gently-aged abode it is today. Indeed, White took two years just to decide on the right person for the restoration, such was her dedication to the place. Like many visionaries, she chose to do much of the initial work herself, before finally employing a stonemason to stamp his professional touch on the façade. Even then, she lugged barrow after barrow of stone up from the paddock to create the now famous paved paths and dry stone walls. These stones were used to reconstruct much of the property, from the buildings to the pavings and garden steps, and the romance of them, with their understated colour and texture, only enhances the beauty of this place, like horticultural cheekbones creating a sophisticated structure for the property's photogenic lines.

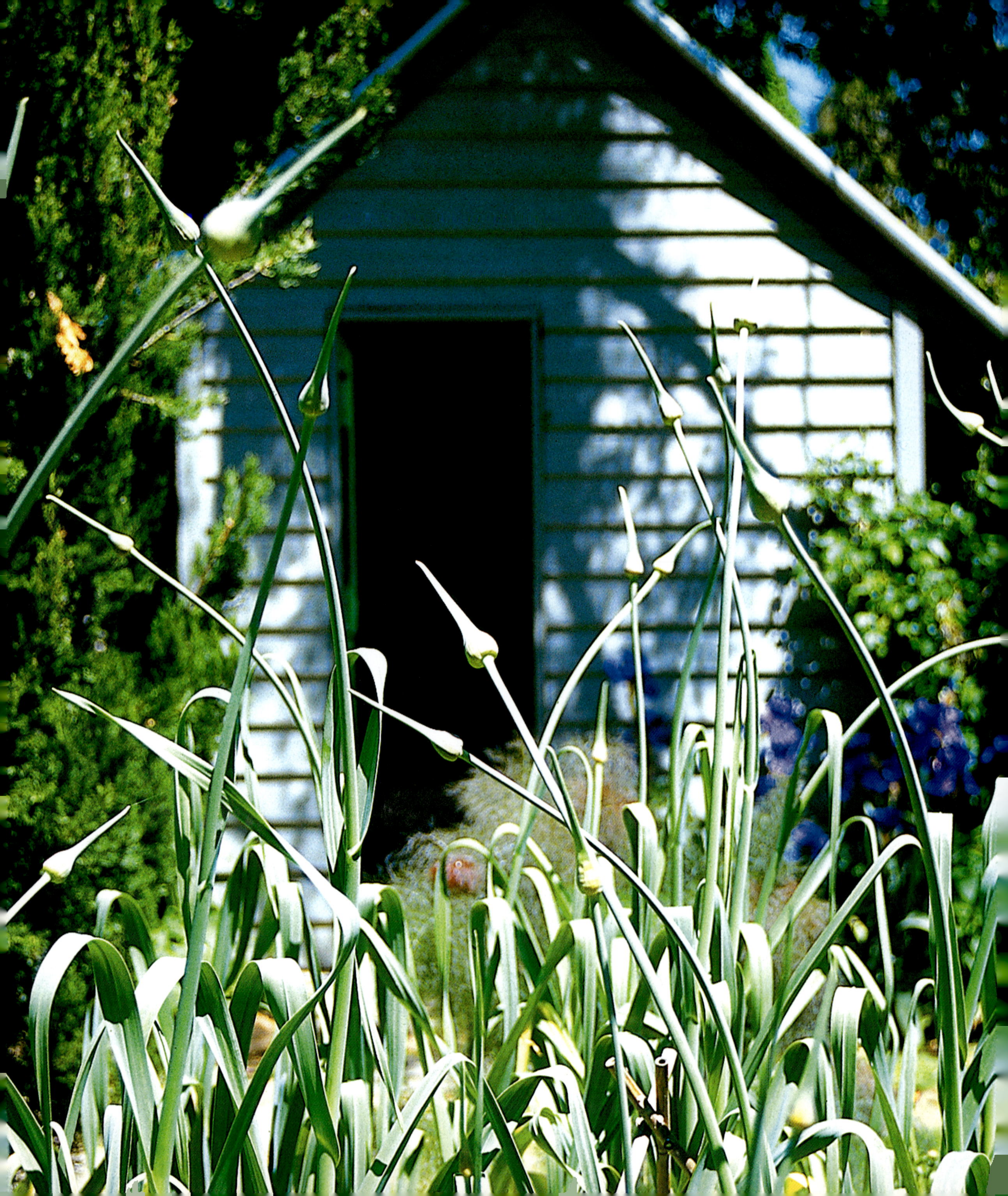

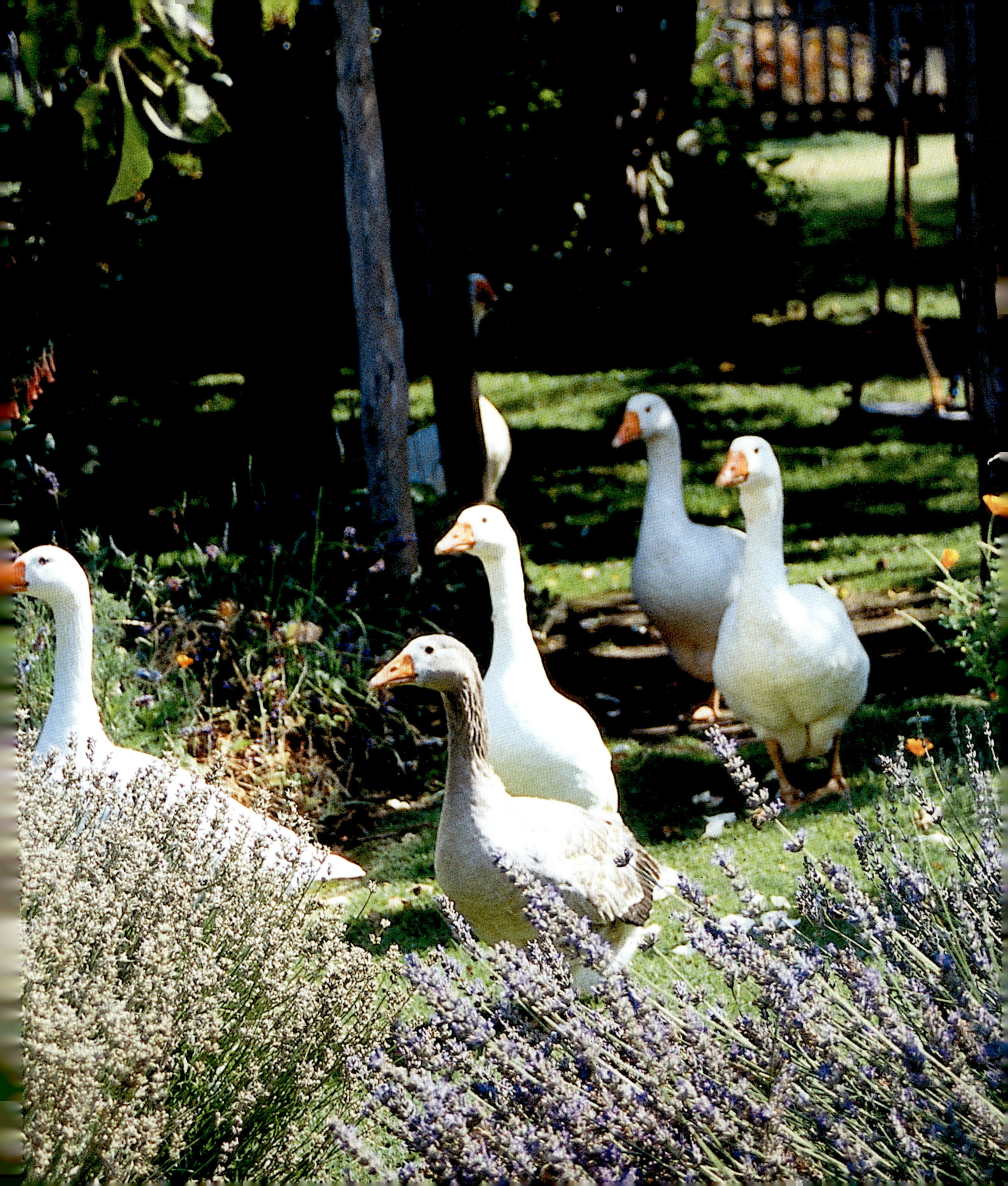

Signs of country life: Lavandula is punctuated with enchanting bits and pieces, from the handsome looking scarecrow to the rustic stone cottages that pepper the property, making it seem more like Tuscany or Provence than Hepburn Springs.

The most enchanting thing about Lavandula is the lavender, after which the property is named. Shaped into great, glorious swathes that are then trimmed into voluminous, sculptural topiary, these purple parterres are equally as beautiful in winter and autumn as they are in summer and spring. But while the property is extraordinary all through the year, it is during summer that the lavender really comes into its own. It is then that the *Lavandula x intermedia* ('Miss Donnington'), among other types, grows prolifically, creating acres of elegant mauve rows that fill the air with heady scent. These lavender fields are harvested each year and turned into oil and body products that are then sold in the 'barn' store. Even the café, La Trattoria, which specialises in some northern Italian cuisine using seasonal produce, sprinkles lavender liberally through its menu, with the lavender lemonade a huge seller amongst those seeking shade under the ash grove or in the stone loggia during summer.

It is a dramatic property; a theatrical collection of perfectly designed lavender fields hemmed by cypress and accessorised by a scattering of potagers and farm animals that could have been created by *Moulin Rouge's* Catherine Martin or Baz Lurhman, had they decided to venture into garden art. And in summer, when the wooden fences drip with a natural embroidery of pink roses and the plump white geese cackle their way around the place, searching for food or shade, there could surely be no more enthralling place in the whole of Australia.

COUNTRY ESTATES

Lavender is an herb rich in history and culture. In medieval times a cross made of lavender hung over the door provided a safeguard against disease and evil. In Tudor times, it came to be associated with love, and newlyweds would put bunches of lavender under their mattress to guarantee marital passion. Today, lavender is widely used to ease stress, depression, hangovers, exhaustion or tension, although romantics still know the value of it as the herb of love.

LAVANDULA

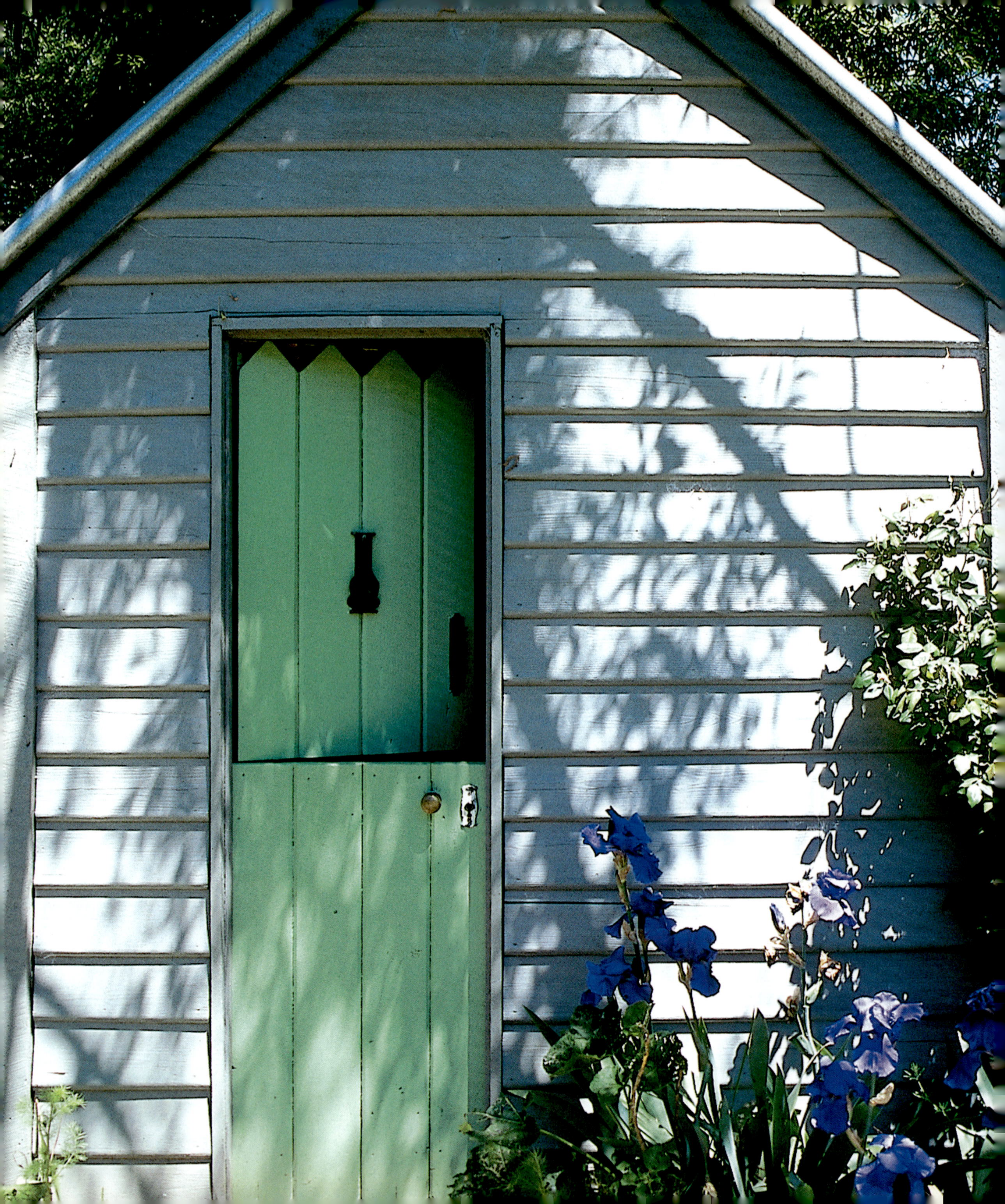

Since the modern world and its myriad deadlines placed a pressure cooker of worry in front of us, many of us have been looking for a way to escape – both physically and psychologically. A country cottage, cabin or even a rustic stone hut like those at Lavandula represents the ultimate private hideaway – a place to retreat from life and all its 'white noise' and remember the value of silence again. The best cottages and cabins, in this respect, are usually the ones hidden well off the beaten track, where the natural beauty of the countryside and the back-to-basic design of the building combine to create a haven for respite and reflection.

LAVANDULA

LEMON POLENTA FLAN

INGREDIENTS

500g butter, softened
500g castor sugar
zest and juice of 3 lemons
zest and juice of 1 orange
7 large organic eggs
1/2 pod of vanilla bean, halved and seeds scraped
550g slivered almonds, crushed to resemble rough breadcrumbs
300g good quality course polenta (use the Moretti brand from Italy)
2 tablespoons baking powder

Pre-heat oven to 170C. Grease six individual flan ramekins, (2cm deep x 20cm), place on baking tray and set aside. In a mixer beat butter, sugar and zests together until thick and pale, then gradually add eggs one at a time beating well after each addition. On a low speed add remaining ingredients, mix thoroughly on a higher speed so that all ingredients are well combined. Place batter into each flan. (Try not to play around with it too much as it is very messy.) The batter will fall to the sides when it is in the oven absorbing the heat. Place in oven and bake on 170C for 35 minutes, until firm to touch. Leave to cool slightly then serve (in the ramekins) with marscapone and raspberries fresh from the garden with a splash of vin santo wine.

Recipe courtesy of Jess Scarce at Lavandula.

EASY CHEESECAKE

INGREDIENTS

half packet of digestive biscuits
1 tin condensed milk
125g cream cheese
(ie Kraft Philadelphia)
1 lemon

Pour the biscuits in a bowl or bag and crush them to a powder with a rolling pin. Press the dough into the bottom of a greased pie dish. Mix together the tin of condensed milk with the cream cheese. Squeeze in the juice of one lemon and whisk together for another 20 seconds. Pour into the pie dish. Leave in the fridge to set. Serve with fresh blueberries.

Lavandula's productive gardens supply the farm's café with fruit, grapes, olives and vegetables. Herbs and green leaves are also picked daily. As country tradition dictates, everything that can be used is used – so the leftovers are made into jams, pickles, chutneys, cordials and sauces. The olives are also pickled, and made into delicious oils.

COUNTRY ESTATES

LAVANDULA

Kennerton Green

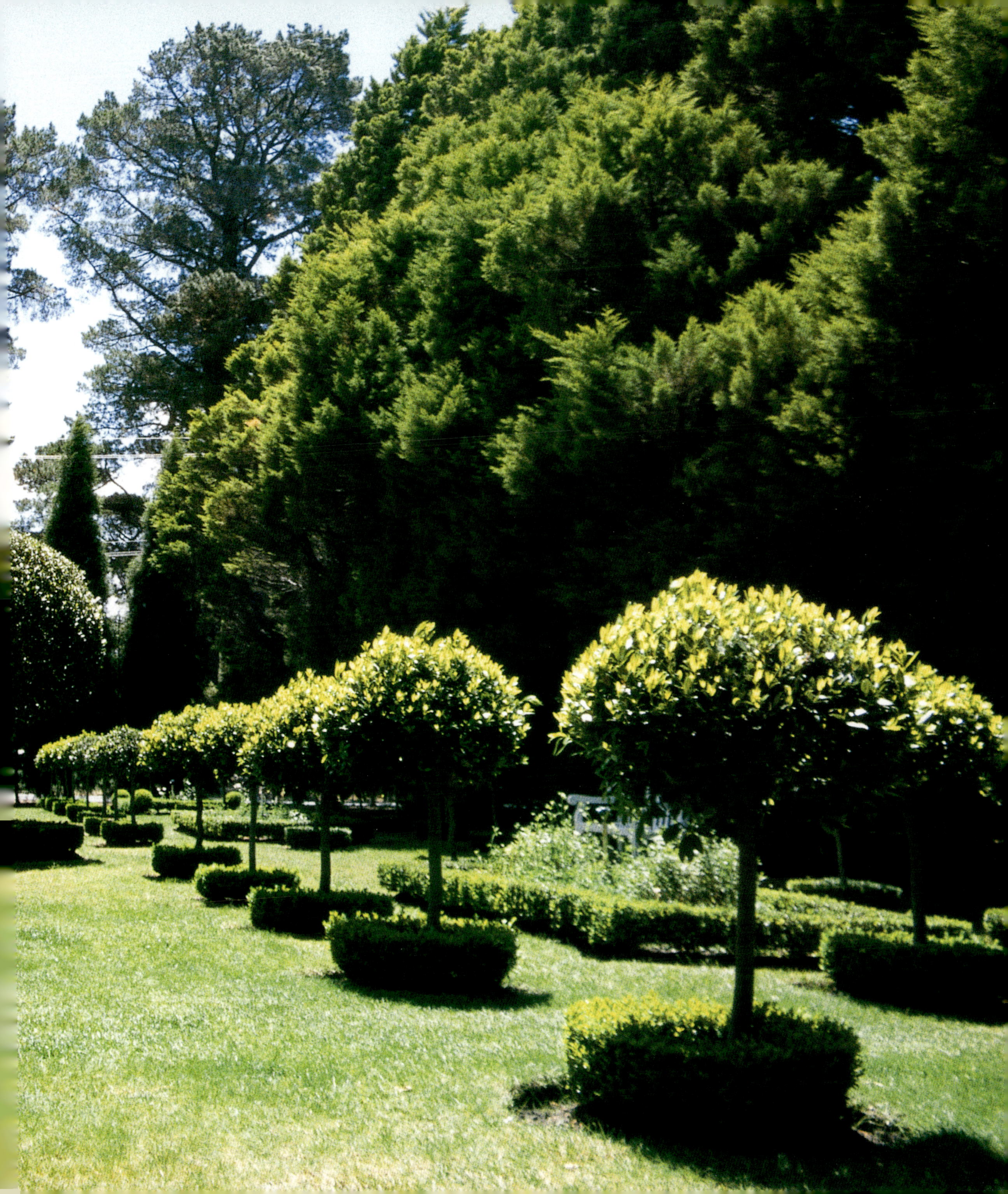

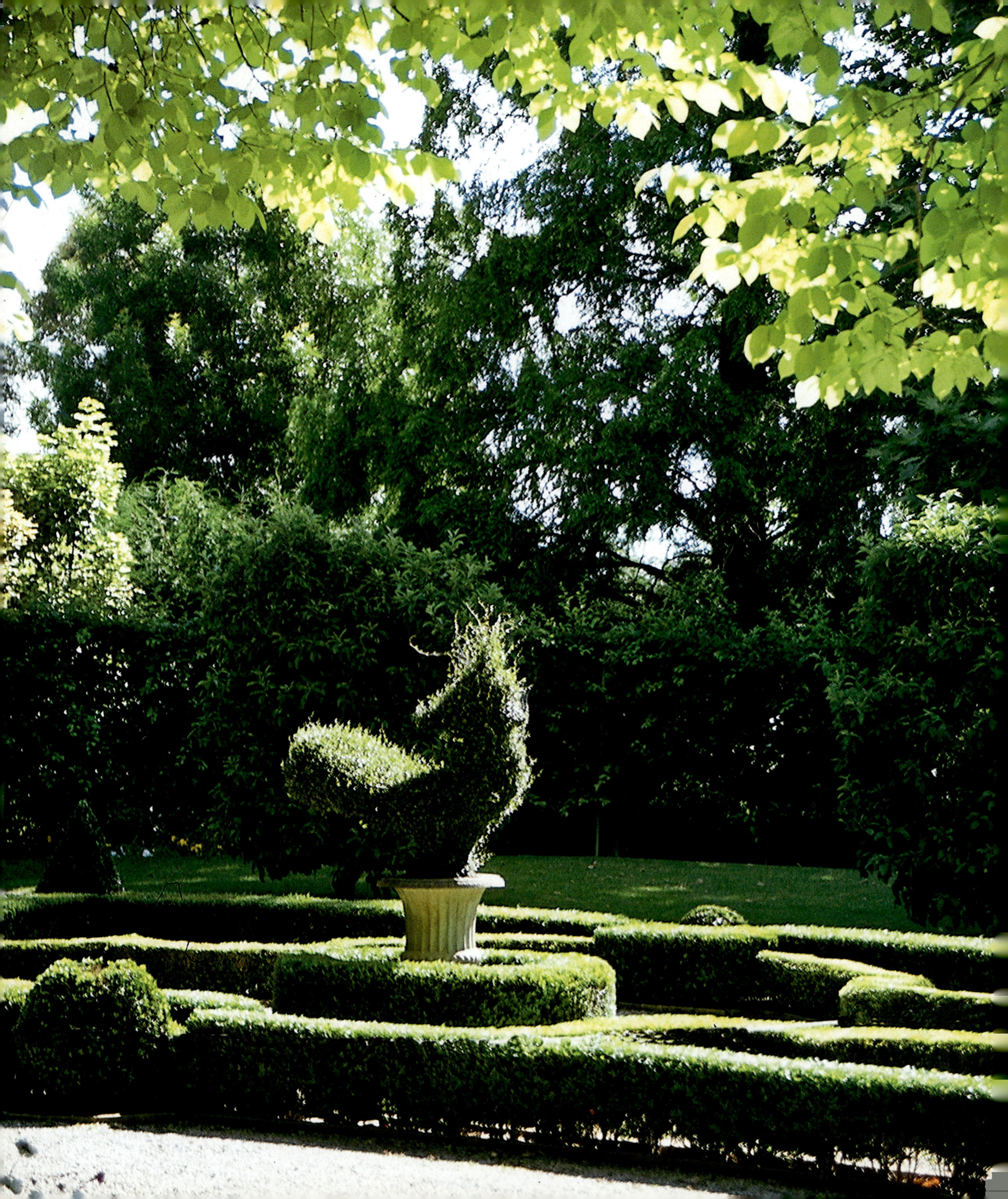

If there is one place that inspires the same glazed-eyed reverence as Sissinghurst in England or Villandry in France, it is Kennerton Green, one of Australia's most extraordinary country properties. The former home of Sir Jock and Lady Pagan, and then, for a short time, Lady Susan Renouf, this sublime corner of the world is so beautiful it has become something of a Mecca for garden lovers, who make the pilgrimage to New South Wales' Southern Highlands each spring to pay their respects – and perhaps also pick up a few ideas of their own. At times the property shimmers with such exquisite perfection it looks like it has been lifted straight from a canvas. Indeed, it is a perfect horticultural example of the famous quote by maverick French artist Marcel Duchamp: 'all is art'.

The bay garden – designed as a 'modern parterre' by current owner Marylyn Abbott – is an impressive ode to the art of topiary, with 80 bay trees trimmed into beautifully disciplined spheres, while the lake is a Monet painting, framed by a frothy garland of delicate, Pompadour pink roses – a spectacular sight on sunny days when the pink petals form a reflection in the pale green surface. The vegetable garden, meanwhile – a true potager in every sense of the term – is a French-inspired fantasy featuring sculptural artichokes, plump strawberries and vivid red-stemmed chard planted in a design so visually pleasing you just want to stay there for hours, watching the light and butterflies drift over the borders.

Abbott, who purchased the property in 1988, is famous for her landscaping talents: she also owns a critically acclaimed garden in England called West Green House, which is renowned for its decorative potager and neoclassical park dotted with follies and bird cages.

At Kennerton Green, she has significantly changed the bones of the original property, introducing geometric beds, well-defined borders and a sense of order and proportion, plus, of course, a whole new series of enchanting garden 'rooms' enclosed within strong architectural hedges of cypress and box, all of which have created a country idyll that offers tantilising vignettes of natural beauty everywhere you turn.

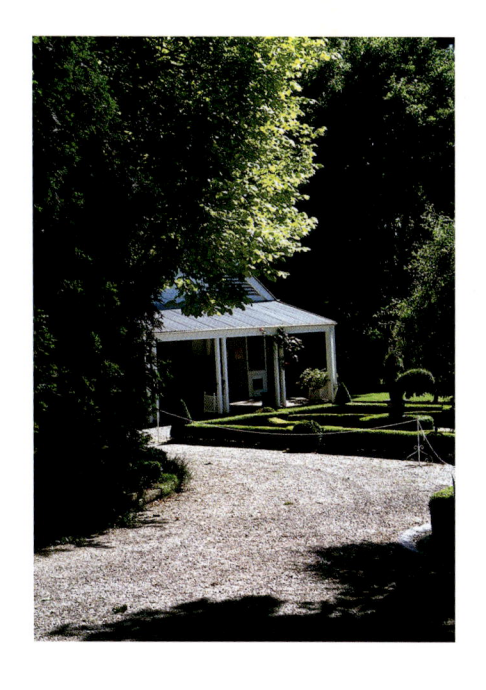

The buildings dotted around Kennerton Green, including the main cottage, top, the peacock house in the potager, left, and the pigeon coop near to to it, are designed to sit in sympathy with the garden, both in terms of their design and in the materials used.

It is a garden where form and function merge seamlessly together, just as good architecture should. But while Kennerton Green is full of bold sight lines and firm axes, it is also notable for its soft curves and almost feminine forms. 'It is an inward looking garden,' said Abbott, describing its unusual style, 'full of gently unfolding surprises.'

At the heart of the property is the house, an 1860s settler's cottage built from white timber that is sweetness redefined. Startlingly small, it is nonetheless perfect for this place because it sits prettily between the pool, with its wisteria and camellia borders, the rose garden, and the elegantly clipped parterre courtyard with its whimsical topiaried bird (shown on page four of this book). A long herbaceous border runs off to one side, and a white gravel driveway curves off to the other. Far from interfering with the lines of the garden, the house actually rests subtly within it; its white façade providing a elegant foil for the sophisticated garden rooms around it.

Once a mostly white garden, Kennerton Green's many corners now feature surprising and delightful accents of colour. One section is devoted solely to flowers in lime tones, another to delicate pinks. Even the potager is planted in carefully coordinated colour schemes, with the lavender, blue kale and chives creating a particularly pretty bed of mauve.

Each garden is designed to inspire a different mood. The pleached circles of Linden trees provoke deep thought, the woodland garden prompts repose, and the potager sweeps you into a feeling of sheer delight. As well, there are statues and bird cages dotted throughout the property that enhance the 'surprise' element. A shepherdess – made in Toulouse, France, in the 18th century – invites you to pause and take in her antique beauty, while an English Regency bird cage, positioned dramatically in the middle of the pond, forces you to stop and stare, breathless, at its theatrical form.

But perhaps the most daring, most delightful corner of the garden is the potager, which is influenced by the great jardin potagers of France. Here, the entrance is via a sublime peacock house and lynch gate, its design copied from the local Bowral church of St Simon and St Jude. Set out in the traditional style and incorporating many of the elements recorded in medieval potagers, it is the exclamation point in a property full of prose: a fitting tribute to a woman who refuses to draw the line at 'ordinary'.

KENNERTON GREEN

Potagers, or ornamental kitchen gardens, first became popular during medieval times when monks, herbalists and anyone else who lived off the land cultivated vegetable gardens in the corners of their abbeys, priories or homes to provide food for the kitchen staff. By and large, they were neat, geometric gardens usually bordered by wattling (a simple weaving of saplings), rustic willow twigs and other beautifully utilitarian materials. Each was carefully constructed into a patterned grid designed to make the most of each vegetable's colour and texture, and the result was produce that was elevated from the merely edible into the astonishingly ornamental.

Today's potager followers, such as Marylyn Abbott and Sir Terence Conran, are now going back to these medieval practices and implementing them in their modern gardens, designing tightly-controlled planting schemes to retain that monastically simple elegance. The best potager vegetables, for those who want to create their own artistic combinations of flavour, are rhubarb, artichokes, red drumhead cabbages, green peppers, beans, squash and pumpkins. Strawberries and espaliered apples can also look effective planted between each section. Ideally, all the produce should be planted in precise lines rather than a ramshackle fashion – real potagers look like a well-designed Amish quilt rather than an old-fashioned veggie patch – and divided by fine gravel paths, which act as the 'bones' of the garden, adding visual drama as well as easy access.

COUNTRY ESTATES

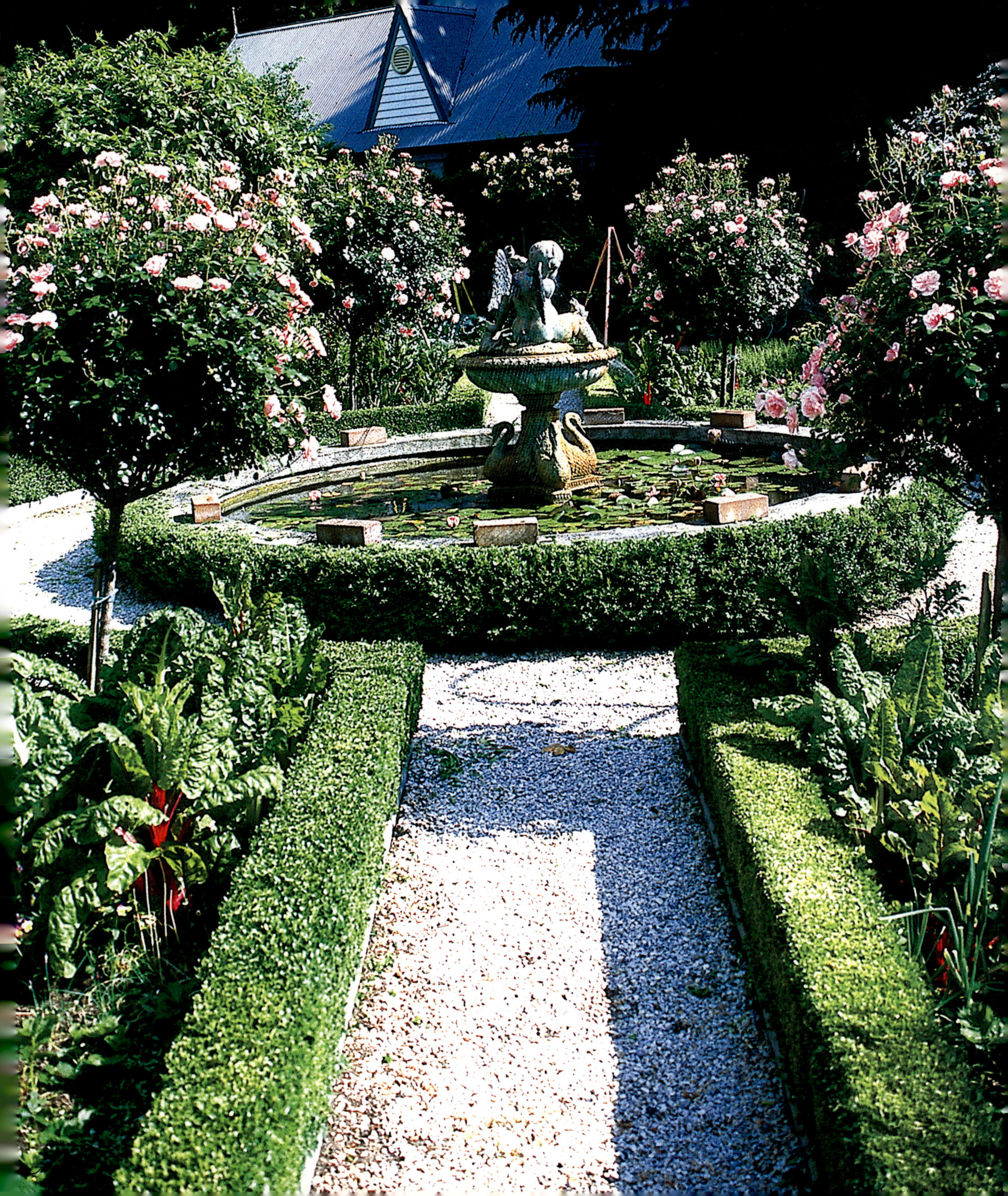

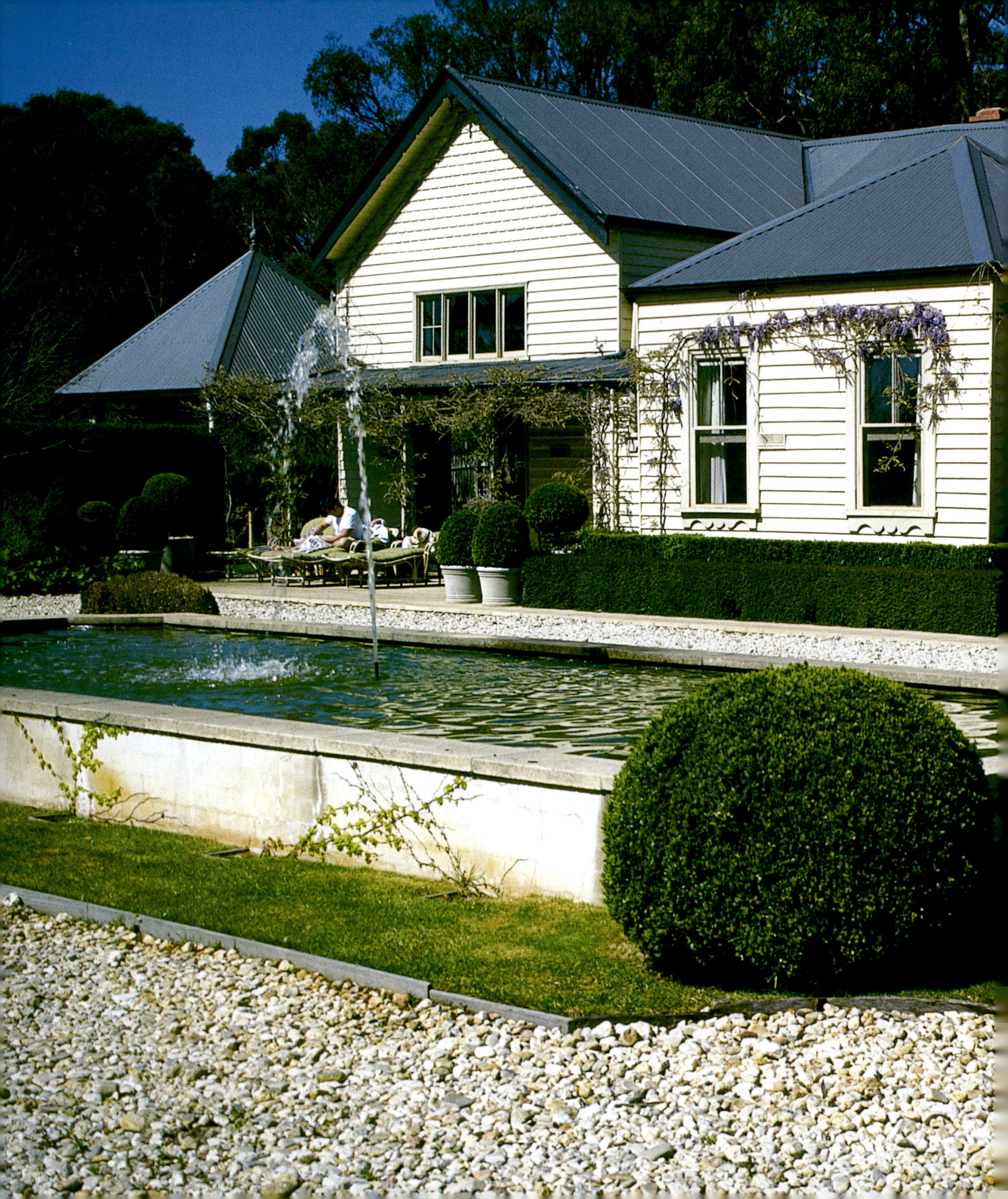

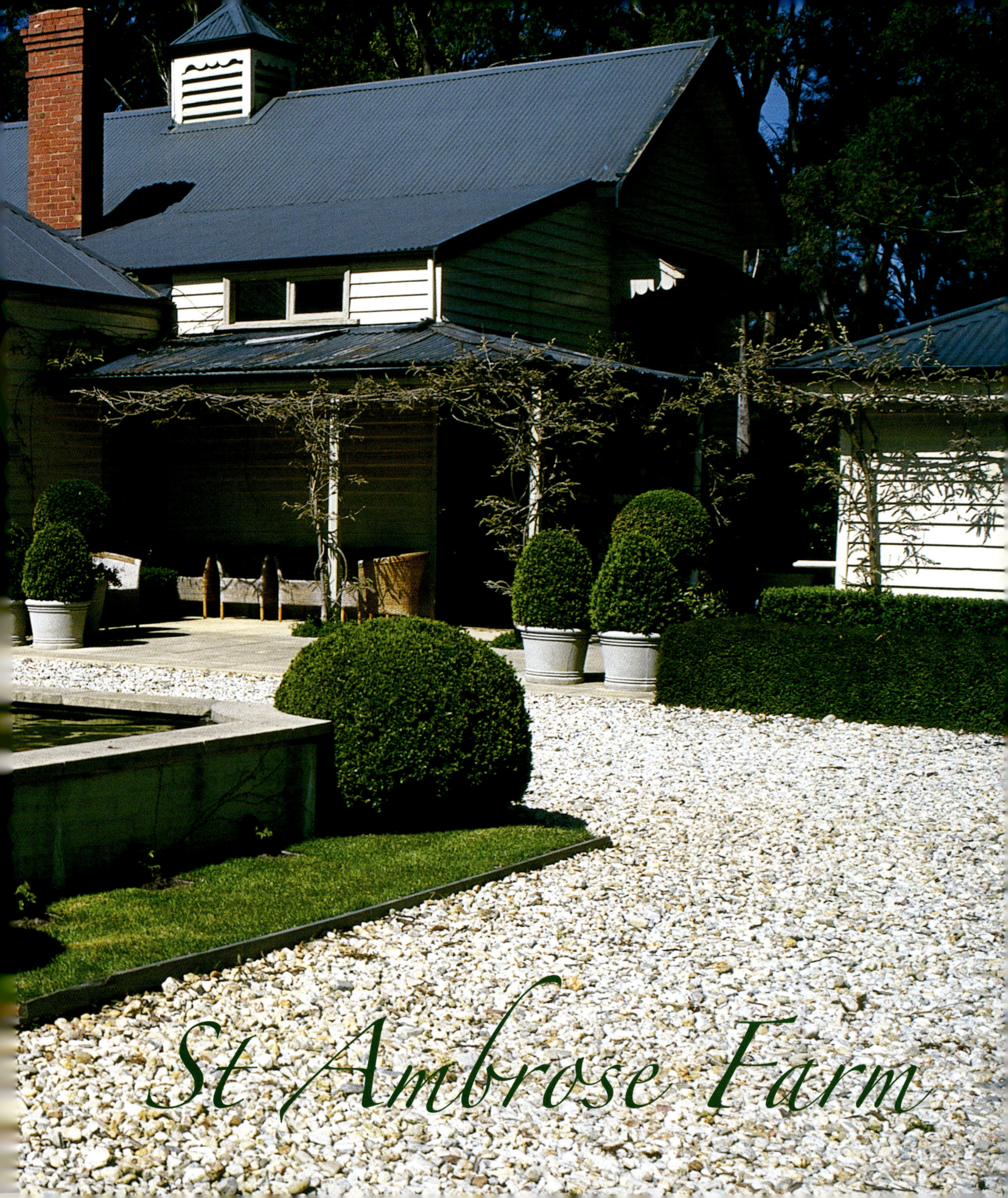

St Ambrose Farm

Landscape designer Paul Bangay is known as the king of clipped hedges, and it's easy to see why: the man can fashion an English box like no other.

If there one person who has proven that a country property can be profitable, it's Paul Bangay. The talented Melbourne-based celebrity gardener has not only made a spectacular showcase of his landscaping skills out of St Ambrose Farm, in the tiny Victorian country town of Woodend, he has made what society queens have rumoured to be a spectacular profit as well.

But money isn't why people move to the country. In fact, it's the last reason people move to the country, because it usually takes a lot of it to restore a rural hideaway. People choose to move to the country for the fresh air, the peace, the greenery, and the gardens. And St Ambrose Farm is a glorious example of all four.

The former schoolhouse, which was built in 1911, was fairly 'utilitarian', to use a diplomatic term, when Bangay bought the property in 1997. Indeed, the building had grown dilapidated with age, and the school ground was little more than dry paddock of weeds. But Bangay, who has made his name by improving the lot (the front lot and the back) of some of Australia's wealthiest and most stylish homeowners, wasn't deterred. He knew he could fashion the former school into a beautiful country retreat: one that would provide a 'living portfolio' of his landscaping talents as much as a tranquil place to get away.

COUNTRY ESTATES

St Ambrose Farm is true garden art – a fitting tribute to the green-fingered talents of its owner Paul Bangay, a truly extraordinary landscape designer.

ST AMBROSE FARM

The pavilion, far right, is the piece de résistance at St Ambrose Farm. An architectural link between inside and out, it is one of the most used 'rooms' in the place. Indeed, some visitors, intending to wander down to the pool with their coffee and papers, stop to rest here and never get up again.

So he sold his cottage in the city, moved his things into his Melbourne office, and travelled up to Woodend on weekends to begin the long process of renovation.

'For the first 12 months I did it myself, going up whenever I could to toss out the junk. Staying there was more like camping!' he says, laughing at the memory. He channelled all his spare funds into the project, and eventually, after many long hours and much hard labour, the promise of what St Ambrose Farm could be started to show through.

The old schoolhouse was converted into a New England-inspired hideaway, with an interior that was almost Shaker-ish in its simplicity, while the garden grew, with a little help from its owner, into a theatrical display of greenery, line, form and life.

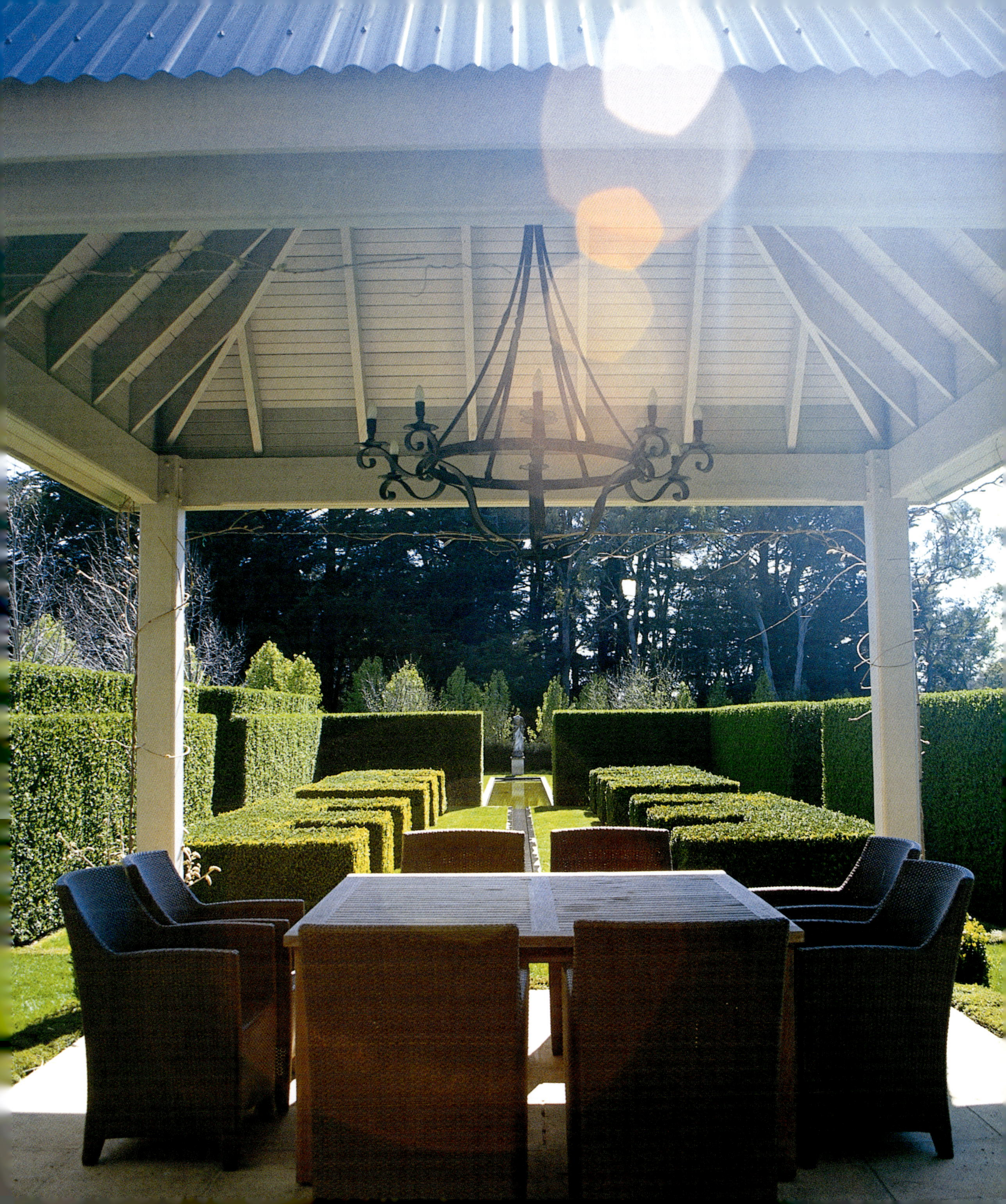

There is an almost Shaker-style simplicity about the interior of the newly renovated schoolhouse at St Ambrose Farm. It's as if the building's stern lines suit the fiercely formal design of the surrounding garden.

In terms of architectural challenges, the schoolhouse – a classic Edwardian country school with a front verandah at one end, three big schoolrooms in the middle and two small rooms at the front – offered more hurdles than most renovations for its new owner. For a start, there were the 6.5-metre wood-lined ceilings, which, although beautiful, could easily make the building feel cold, especially during Woodend's fiercely cold winter days. There was also a great deal of rot that had set in during the school's long period of neglect. But, determined to maintain the school's character and dignity, Paul set about fixing the problems while working out how to make the most of the rooms.

In the end, he decided to simply retain the original floorplan, rather than remove internal walls or add extensions. The modesty of it all resulted in a floorplan that was so simple, it was beautiful – and surprisingly elegant.

The final changes that were made were minimal, and included French doors (which helped bring the garden inside) and an opening in the wall between kitchen and living room, to allow for ease of movement as well as light.

Additional inspiration for the interior was provided by Paul Bangay's close friends, interior designers John Coote and Stuart Rattle. (Rattle also owns a property in the country, not far from St Ambrose Farm.) For Bangay, the schoolhouse's interior decoration was just as important as the garden design, because – even for a landscape architect – you need somewhere to come home to at the end of the day.

With the help of these stylish gentlemen, the schoolhouse's once dark and heavy rooms were transformed by a muted colour scheme taken from the natural colour palettes outside the rear windows. Several years on, the decision has proven to be a wise one. The gumtree-inspired greys and beiges certainly suit the new mood of the now glamorous residence, while acting as a subtle foil for the lush green garden that grows prolifically outside. Other natural hues have given life to the rest of the rooms – olive green in the sitting room, gum tree bark grey in the kitchen and khaki on the floors. The exterior was also painted in a similar palette. with the roof finished in a shade of charcoal that echoed the grey of old slates. The former school masters would have approved.

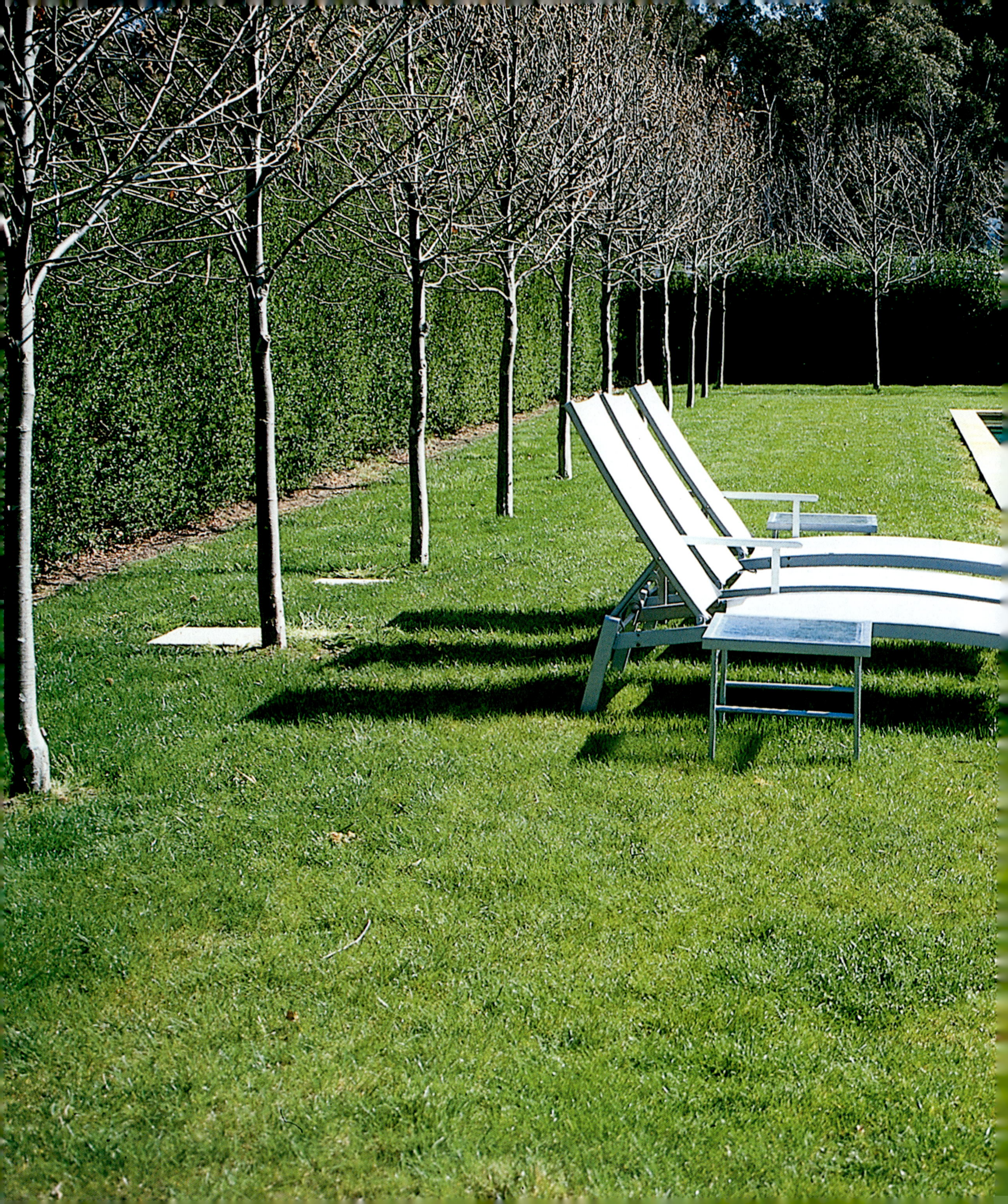

The pool is a study is Bangay-esque symmetry and simplicity. The deliberately elongated shape was designed to mirror the nearby reflection pond, and in doing so suggest an ornamental pond, rather than an ordinary lap pool. The grass-green colour was also deliberate, to reflect the deep green of the surrounding garden. But the real highlight is perhaps the border of pleached plane trees that line the edge of the pool garden, trees that look as elegant in Winter as they do in Spring.

60

After eight years, Paul Bangay decided to sell and start all over again. It's a professional hazard for a landscape architect: there's always another garden, another vision, another project to begin. So St Ambrose was sold in 2005, reportedly to someone who loved it as much as its owner did, and Bangay purchased another block, this time at Kyneton, to create another farm, another garden. When these photos were taken he had even been down to the Royal Melbourne Show to look over some cows for his new country estate. Although reluctant to leave St Ambrose, he knows he has done all that can be done there. Like everything in the country, things must change. And St Ambrose is no exception.

ST AMBROSE FARM

FROZEN WATERMELON, LIME AND RASPBERRY COCKTAIL

INGREDIENTS
1 watermelon
zest and juice of 4 limes
2 punnets raspberries

Put the watermelon and raspberries in a juicer and mix. Add the zest and lime juice. Place in a freezer container and then into the freezer to freeze.

To serve, scoop small balls of the juice into a parfait or cocktail glass. Top with a slice of lime and a sprig of mint and serve with a straw.
If you want a slushie-style drink, blend the frozen juice quickly in a food processor. (Note: It defrosts quite quickly so don't over-process or the juice will simply liquefy.) Splash over a nip of vodka, white rum or grand marnier, for a delicious cocktail.

Adapted from Citrus Deli, Byron Bay.

Formality and informality come together easily at St Ambrose Farm, as shown here with the elegantly casual air of the tree-lined driveway and the more formal but just as fabulous statue that sits proudly in the lower layer of an immaculately clipped hedge.

ST AMBROSE FARM

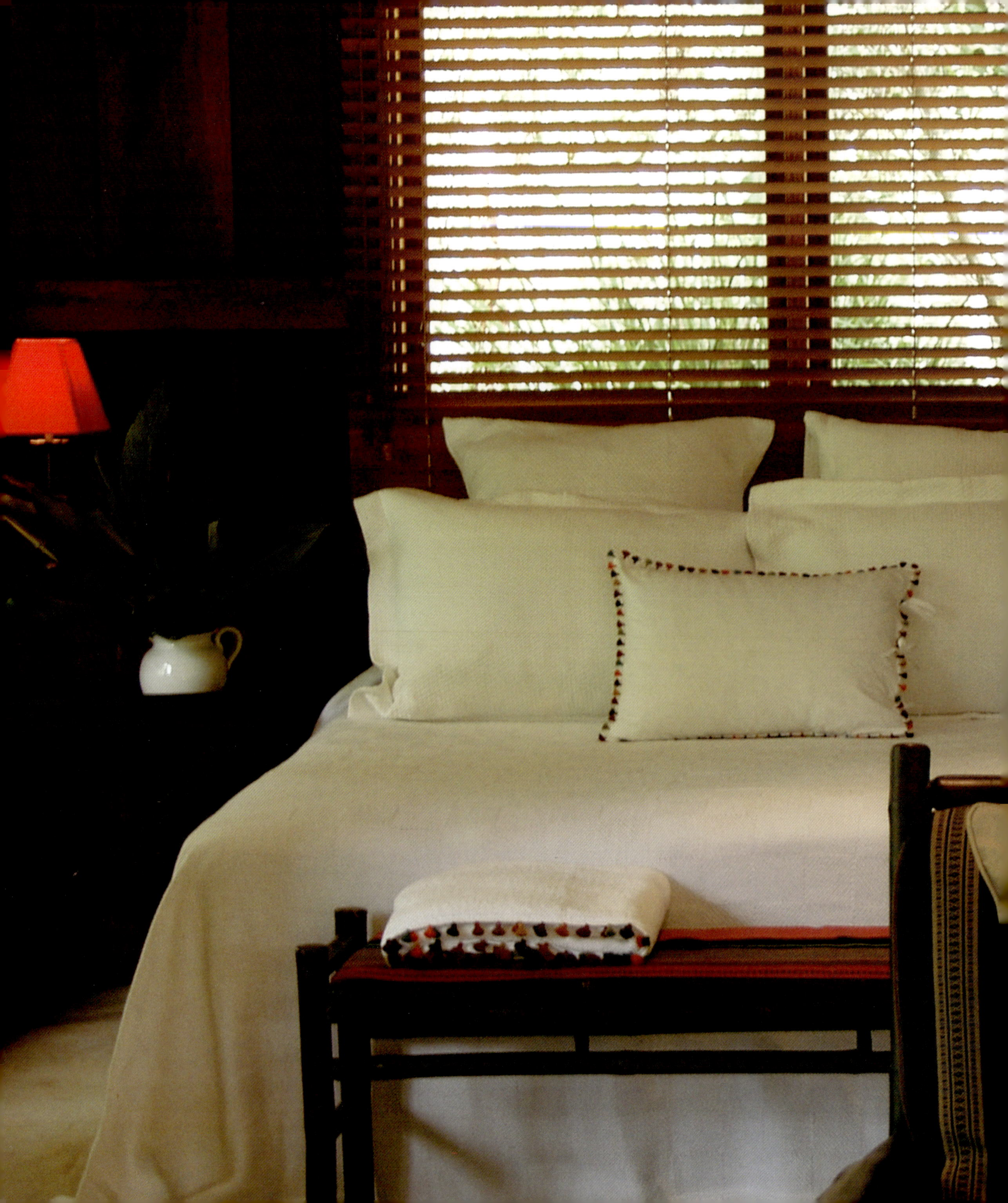

Mulabinba

Country icons, opppsite: Akubra hats and workboots form a distinctly Australian still life on a table fashioned from a slab of weathered timber at the back of a side verandah. It is just one of the many painterly vignettes that form the highly stylised canvas of Anne and Anthony Everingham's home. While they may not realise they are creating art every time they put down a hat or place a chair, this is one couple for whom the art of glamorous living comes completely naturally.

What is it that distinguishes the truly beautiful country houses from the more ordinary ones? Is it the design, the grandeur of the architect's vision? Is it the garden, so much a part of any country property? Or is it simply the style that the owners have imparted on the place, giving a property its character and dignity?

There are many, magazine writers among them, who believe it's the latter. Without a sense of individual style, suggest editors, a country property is simply a dwelling in a picturesque patch of landscape: a couple of walls propped up by some gently aged timber and some soothing views.

At Anne and Anthony Everingham's house, located deep in the hinterland behind Noosa, style infuses just about everything they do, whether it's their decision to upholster the cane couches slung along the cool verandah in a glamourous St Tropez-style charcoal and biscuit-striped French canvas, or their treatment of the garden guesthouse, which is now decorated in an extraordinarily rich (and extraordinarily fabulous) mix of chocolate and chilli red – a dramatic contrast to the deep tropical green of the surrounding garden.

COUNTRY ESTATES

MULABINBA

But then, this is the sort of quiet creativity you'd expect from a family of artists who take as their cue the splashes of natural beauty that rain down on them everyday.

Anne Everingham, a jewellery designer, is the main one responsible for the distinct look of this distinguished *Out of Africa*-style hideaway. It was she who decided to create the guesthouse and studio and it is she who still constantly moves things around, creating vignettes of country life out of objects found in out-of-the-way markets here and overseas.

The living room is perhaps the most enthralling space in this irresistible rural hideaway. A veritable gallery of exotic artifacts, it includes wooden fertility men from Kenya that sit vis-à-vis with wooden candlesticks from China and Istanbul, bone boxes from Masai warriors and a collection of walking sticks from all four corners of the globe.

All of the pieces, whether they're artifacts or furniture, look surprisingly at home in the tropical bush setting thanks to the unifying colour scheme of blacks, blues, reds and greens, which keeps everything sophisticated in a beautifully understated way. From the dramatic bedrooms to the Jacaranda-lined drive, this is one home where style comes, well, completely naturally.

When the Everinghams bought the property in 1981, it was a tiny fibro shack. There were only two bedrooms and a lean-to bathroom. But it had the white posts that are now the centrepiece of the property, and it was these the Everinghams fell in love with, along with the low-slung roof. 'We loved the roof and those posts,' says Anne Everingham. 'The house just had a wonderful feel'.

The guesthouse at the end of the garden was decorated in rich shades of chocolate and chilli red: a treatment that immediately made the interior stand out against the deep greens of the tropical garden (right). The fabric – a striped espadrille-style canvas from the south of France – was sourced from Otilly and Lewis in Peregian Beach, who imported it from Le Toiles de Soleil in Paris. The cost was well worth it: the guesthouse now looks like a luxury hideaway.

COUNTRY ESTATES

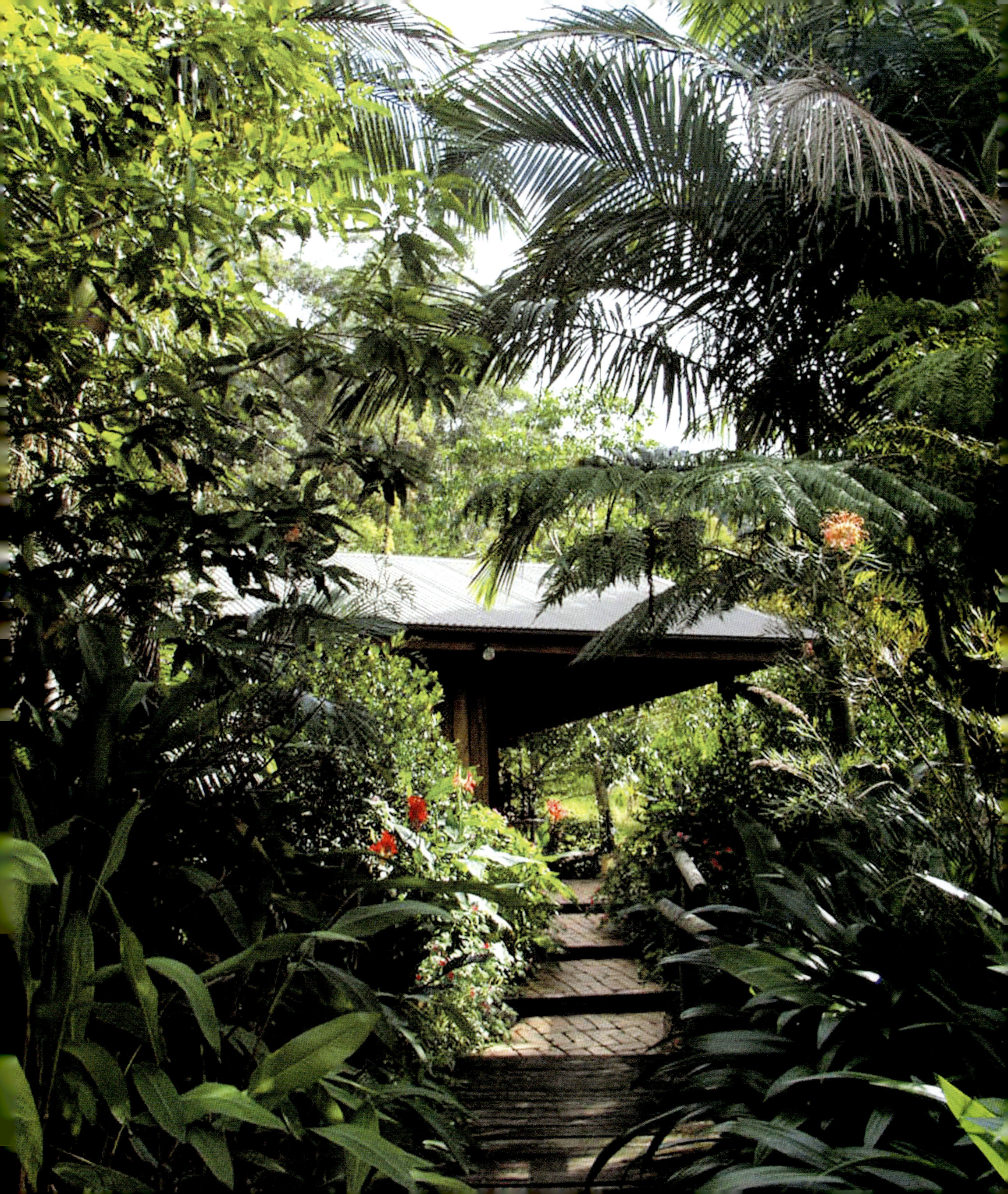

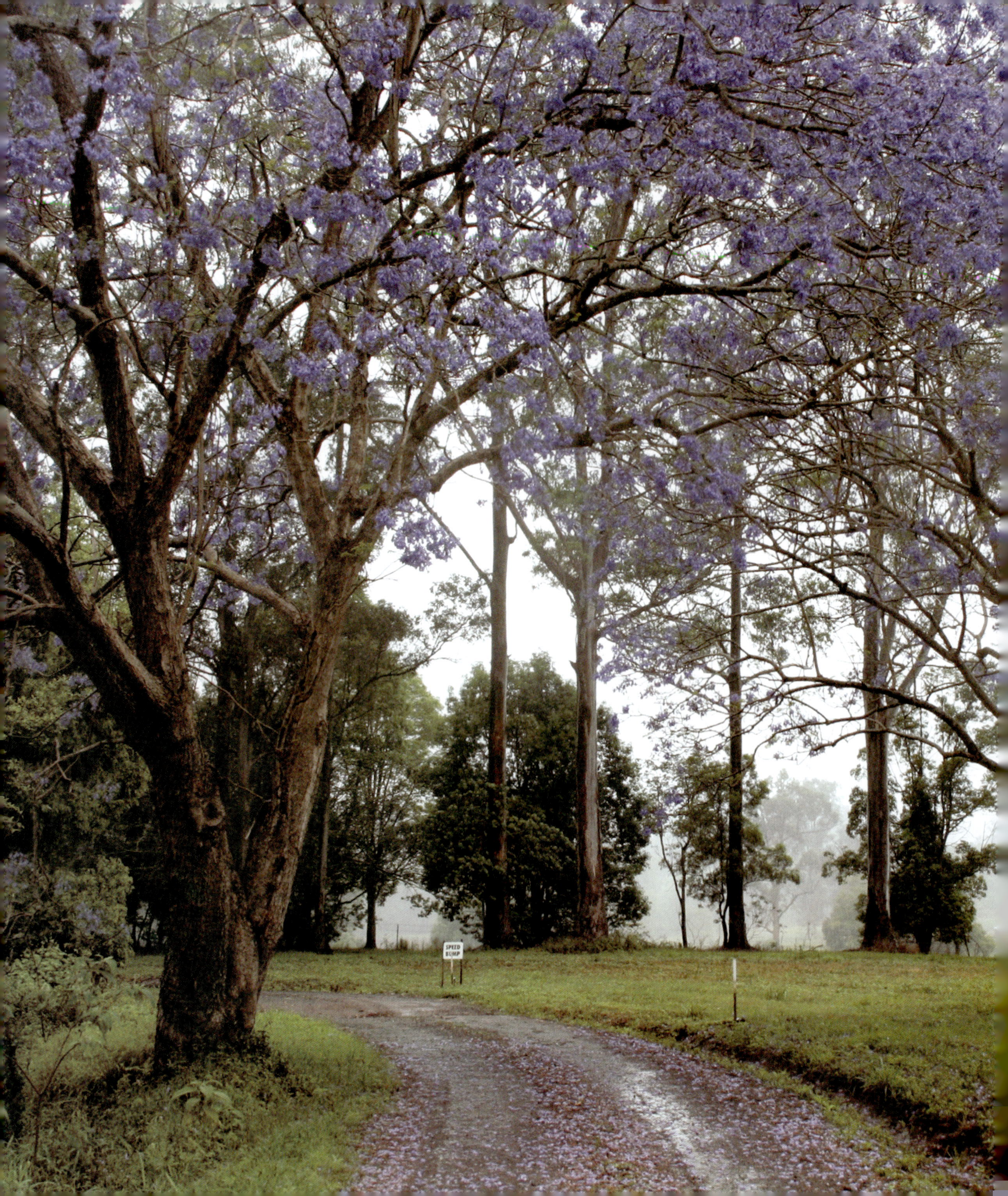
SPEED
BUMP

MULABINBA

Style is part of everyday life at the Everingham's home: the iron cross in Anne Everingham's studio was fashioned by her son, the various platters were brought back from Africa by Anne and her husband, and the bamboo chairs on the verandah are just one part of a chic collection of outdoor pieces that have elevated the verandah to a glamourous entertaining area.

COUNTRY ESTATES

GINGER, DATE AND ALMOND TORTE

INGREDIENTS
250g flaked almonds (lightly toasted)
100g finely chopped glace ginger
150g finely chopped dates
250g chopped dark chocolate
6 egg whites
1/2 cup castor sugar
300ml cream
3 tablespoons ginger liqueur
crystalized ginger to garnish

Beat egg whites until they hold soft peaks. Gradually add castor sugar and continue beating for one minute. Fold in almonds, ginger, chocolate and dates. Pour mixture into a 23cm tin which has been lined with greased foil. Bake in a preheated oven at 170C for 40 to 45 minutes. Turn oven off and allow cake to cool with door open. When cool, turn out onto a platter and garnish.
To garnish, lightly whip cream and add the ginger liqueur, whisk until soft peaks form. Spread onto torte and garnish with chopped crystallised ginger.

RUSTIC PEAR TARTE TARTIN

INGREDIENTS
6 firm pears
100g butter
4 sticks cinnamon
300g brown sugar
100ml fresh lime or lemon juice
2 sheets puff pastry
double cream

Peel, halve and core pears, leaving the stem intact, then lay them rounded side down on a hot buttered frypan with the stems towards the centre. Place cinnamon sticks between them and sprinkle over the sugar and juice. Cook over low heat until pears are brown and soft and the syrup has thickened. Remove the frypan, place the two sheets of pastry over the top of the pears (in frypan) and set the lot in a preheated oven until pastry has cooked. When done, invert the pastry and pears onto a white platter and serve with double cream.

MULABINBA

Spray Farm

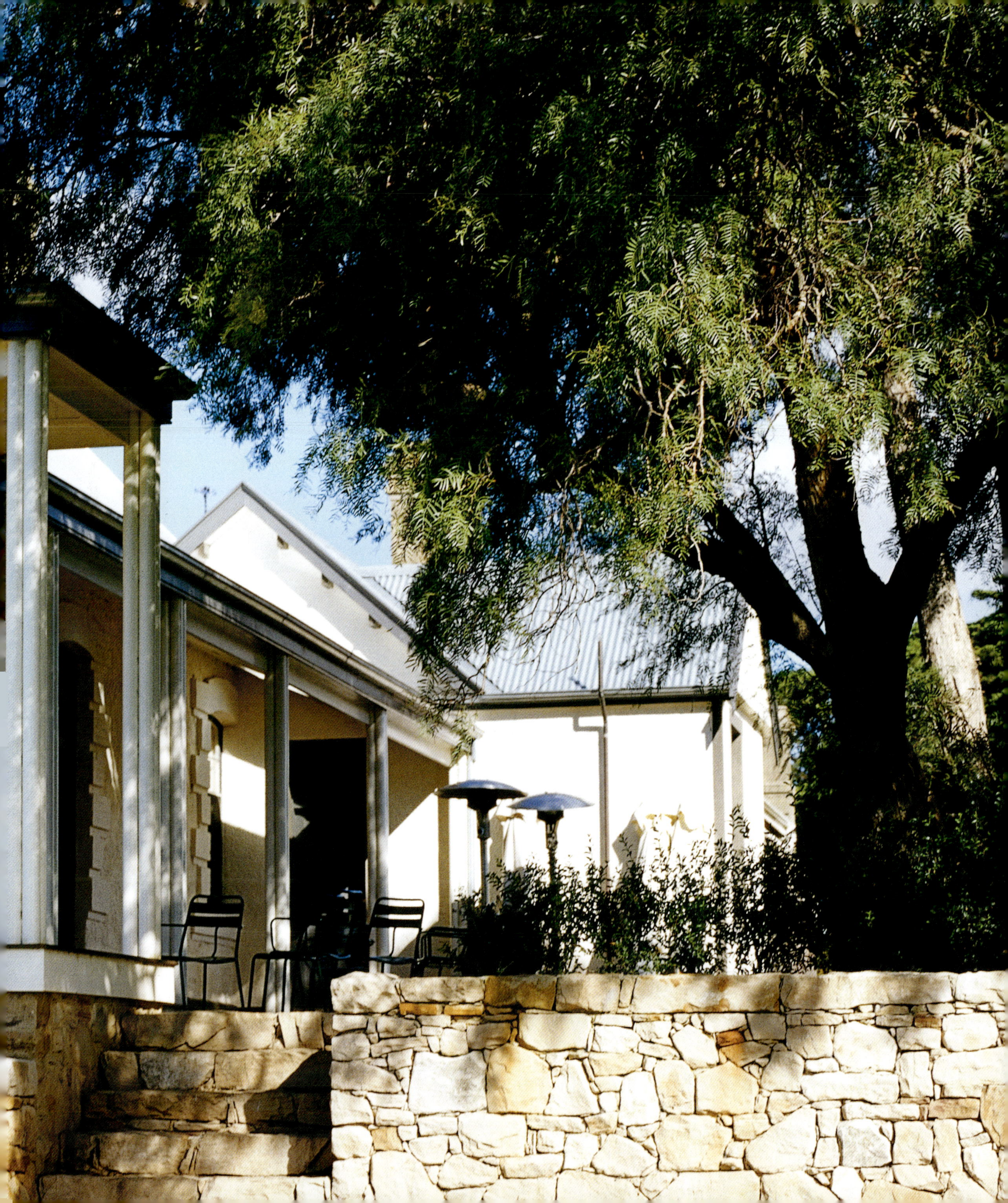

'It is simply the most magical place,' says Paul Bangay, who was commissioned by the Brownes to design the garden surrounding Spray Farm's homestead. 'When you're down there on a still day looking out towards the sea, it is like nothing else'.

Some places ignite the imagination before you've even stepped inside the front gate. Take Spray Farm, for example. Just the name is enough to invoke images of sea views, clucking chooks and veggie patches groaning with produce. But however quaint it sounds, Spray Farm is not your average farm, although there is a veggie garden – a spectacular Paul Bangay-designed patch set neatly beside the stables. And there is a sea view – a great gorgeous sweep of ocean that almost eclipses the house and garden in its beauty. Other than that, this homestead is far from ordinary, and all those who visit recognise the fact immediately.

Located on Victoria's Bellarine Peninsula, the property is owned by winemakers David and Vivienne Browne, whose premium labels Scotchman's Hill and Swan Bay (formerly Spray Farm) are sold here at the cellar door. Purchased in 1994 the semi-derelict, 150-year-old homestead was restored to its former glory by the Brownes after they purchased it at auction. There was a certain serendipity about the sale. As a boy, David Browne had wandered past the old house many times on his exploration of the nearby coast, and had

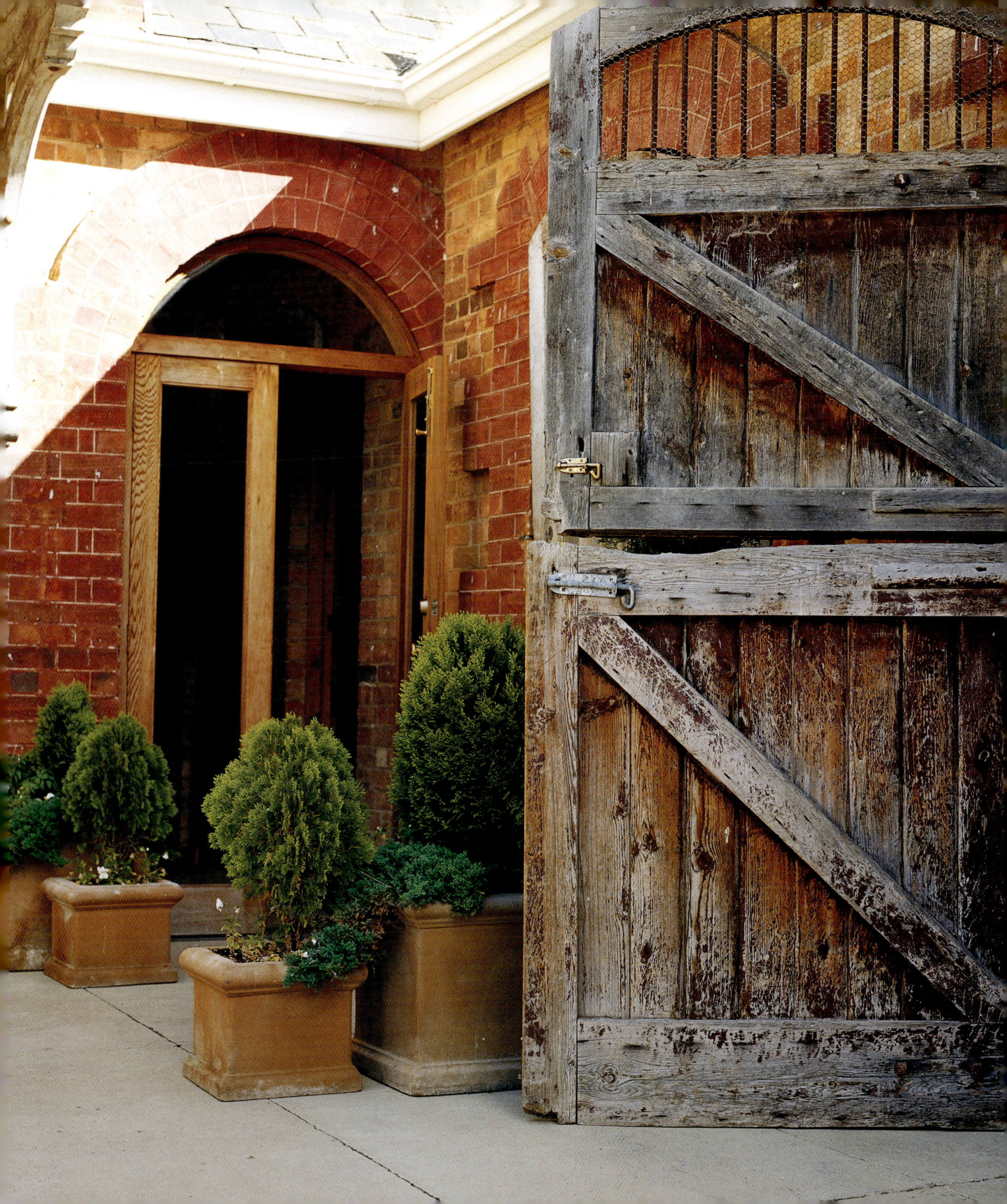

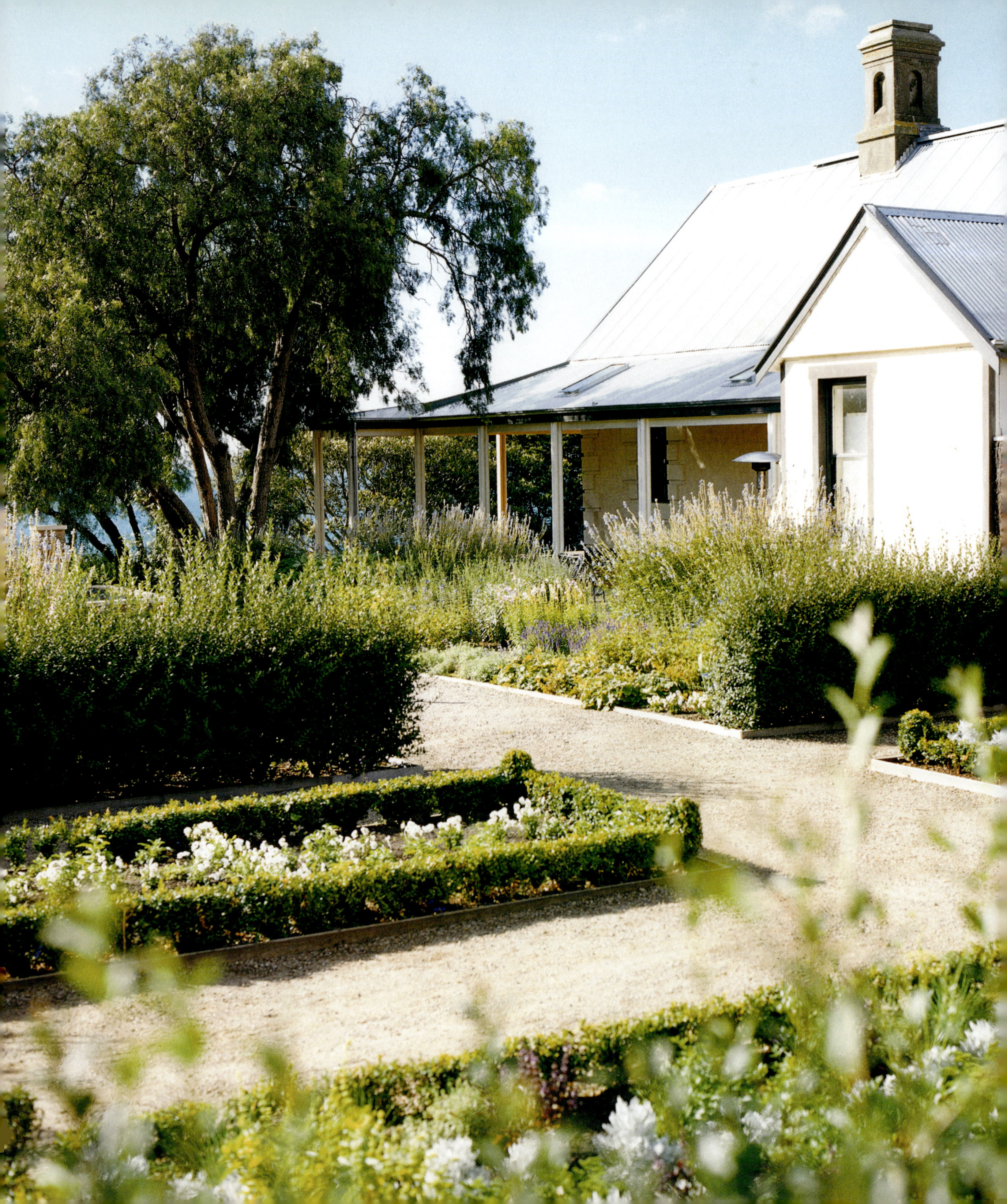

always wandered what would become of it. Years later, after a successful stint as a stockbroker in London and then a winemaker in Australia, he found he had the funds to buy and restore it himself. It was almost as if it was destined to be his.

Now, as you crunch-crunch your way through the white gates, across the gravel driveway and into the courtyard, past the grand old wooden stable doors, the lichen-covered slate roof with its copper weathervane, and the long, thoroughly romantic low-slung verandah, you can see why it was worth saving.

Like the garden, the house, courtyard and stables are all elegantly simple. The house's bluestone façade was repainted in its original off-white colour and trimmed in Abyssinian grey. The enormous stable doors were also retained and given a facelift, which was so successful that any new wooden doors have had to be painted to make them look just as old. 'We've spent a fortune making the whole place look old!' laughs Vivienne Browne. But you get the feeling she doesn't regret it in the least.

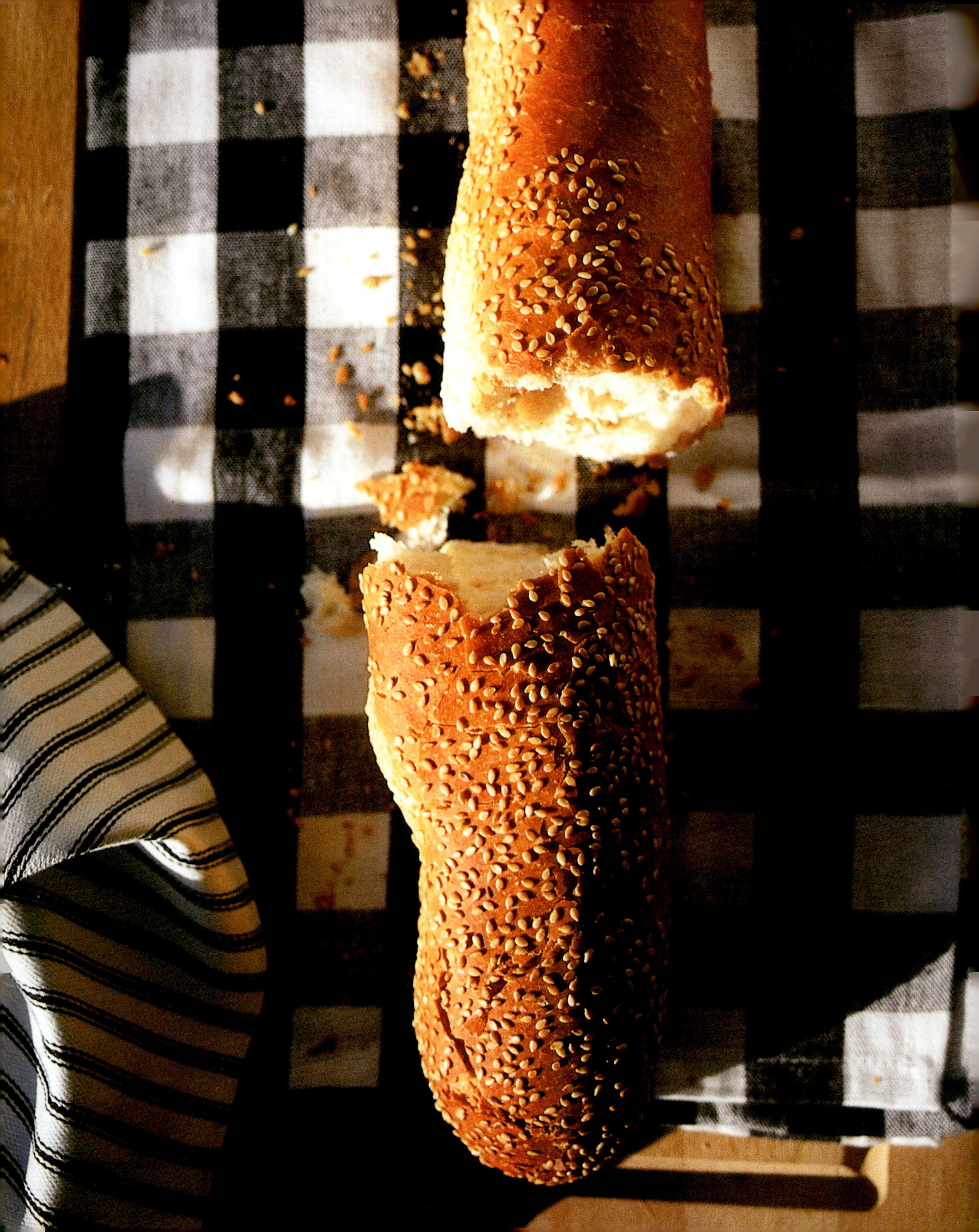

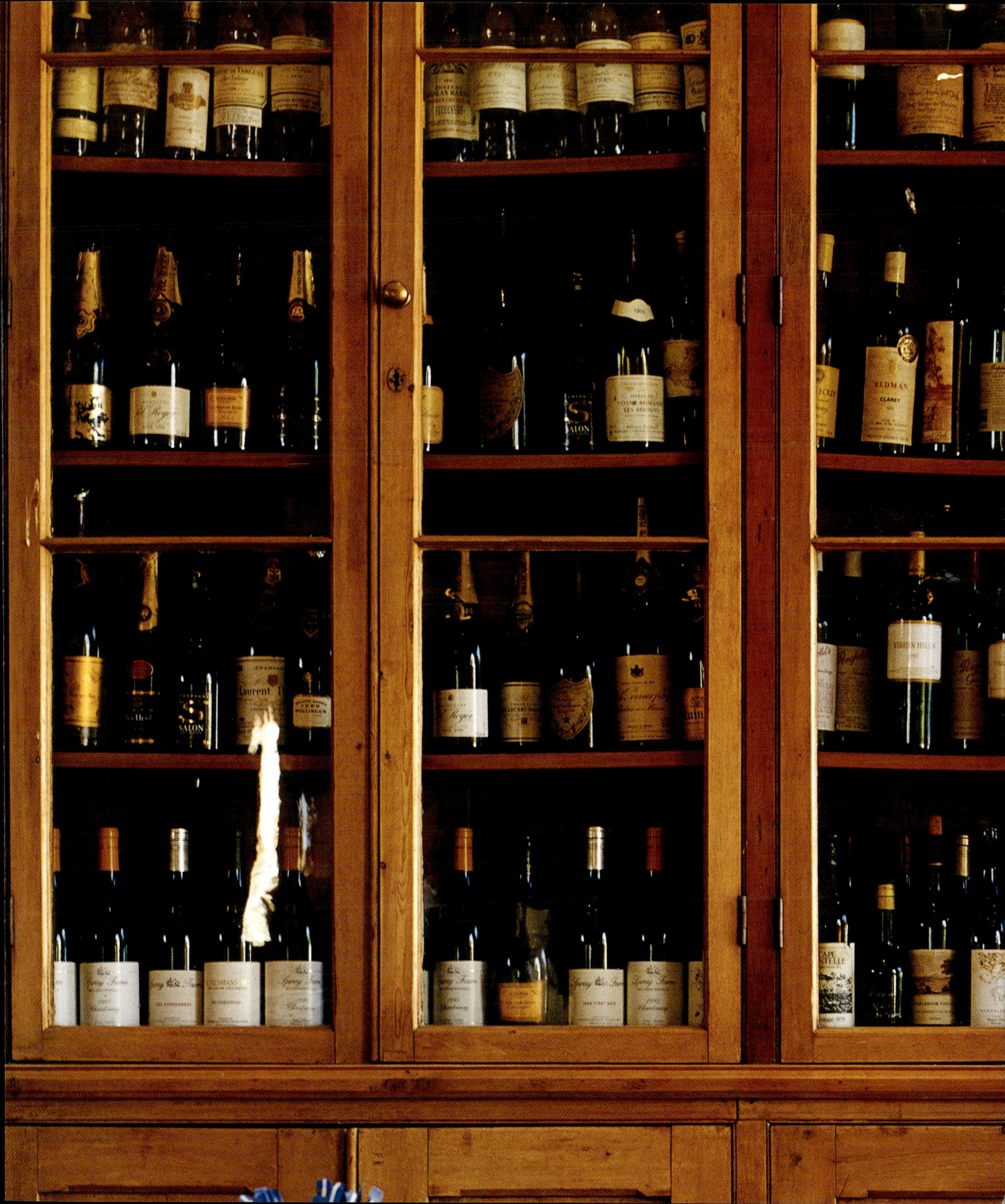
REDMAN
CLARET
VIRGIN HILLS
SALON
BOLLINGER

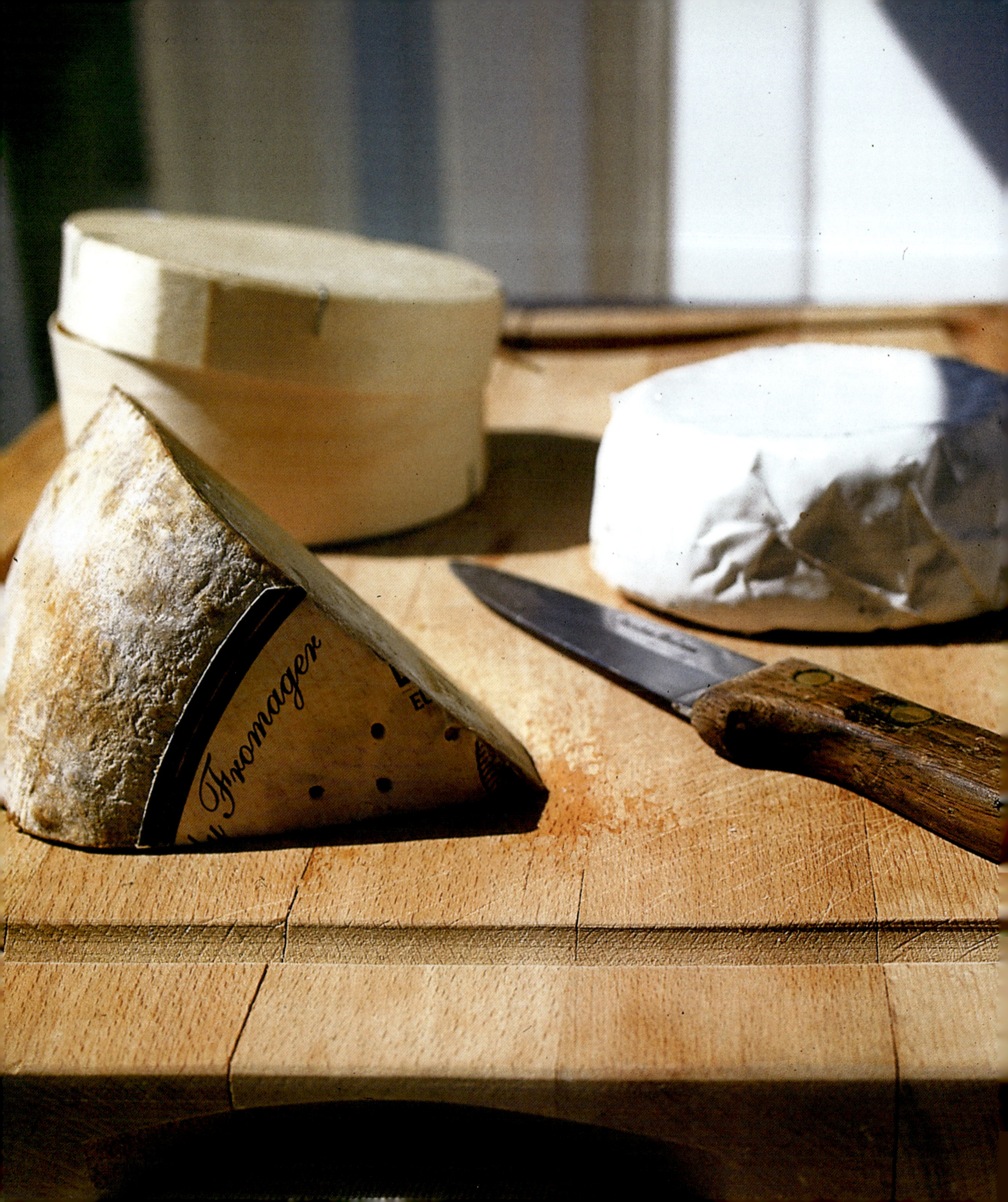
Fromager

POACHED PEARS WITH BLUE CHEESE

INGREDIENTS
2 pears (firm)
2 tablespoons honey
150ml cranberry juice
150ml red wine
200g cranberries
2 cinnamon sticks
5 cloves
200g blue cheese, room temperature
2 tablespoons cranberry sauce,
or cranberry relish

Halve and core pears, and cut into eight wedges. Place in a pan and add honey, cranberry juice and wine (a Swan Bay Pinot Noir is perfect). Simmer for 10-15 minutes, until the pears are tender. Remove pears, drain (keeping liquid) and slice into thin slices. Reduce the liquid and then add the cranberries, and cinnamon. Simmer for another 2-3 minutes. Transfer everything to a small heatproof bowl and leave to cool. Toast some thick bread (sourdough is perfect) and spread each slice with a thick layer of blue cheese. Top with the poached pear slices; spooning over a dollop of cranberry relish to finish. Serve with a big glass of Swan Bay Pinot Noir 2004.

Adapted from an original recipe by Merrilees Parker.

The Brownes decided to change the name of their Spray Farm wine to Swan Bay after discovering that the word 'spray' had negative connotations within the European wine market. The new name, Swan Bay, was taken from the shimmering blue body of water that Spray Farm overlooks. The label, produced by the Browne's Scotchmans Hill Group, is highly regarded, with the 2001 Sauvignon Blanc Semillon especially favoured by wine lovers for its full, rich flavour. Paired with savoury foods, such as Greek mezze platters or mature cheese, it completes a wonderfully light and refreshing summer meal.

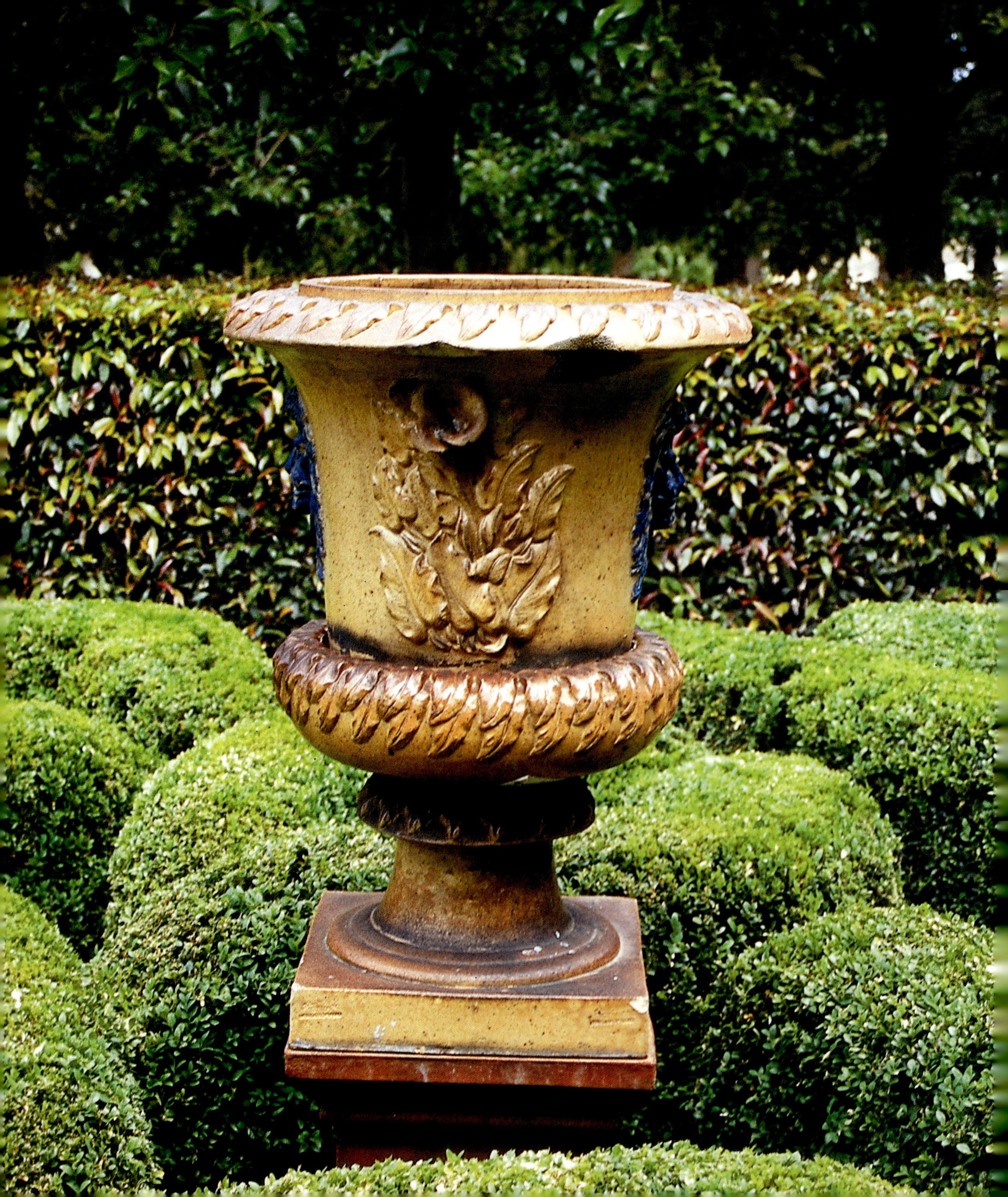

Great Country Houses

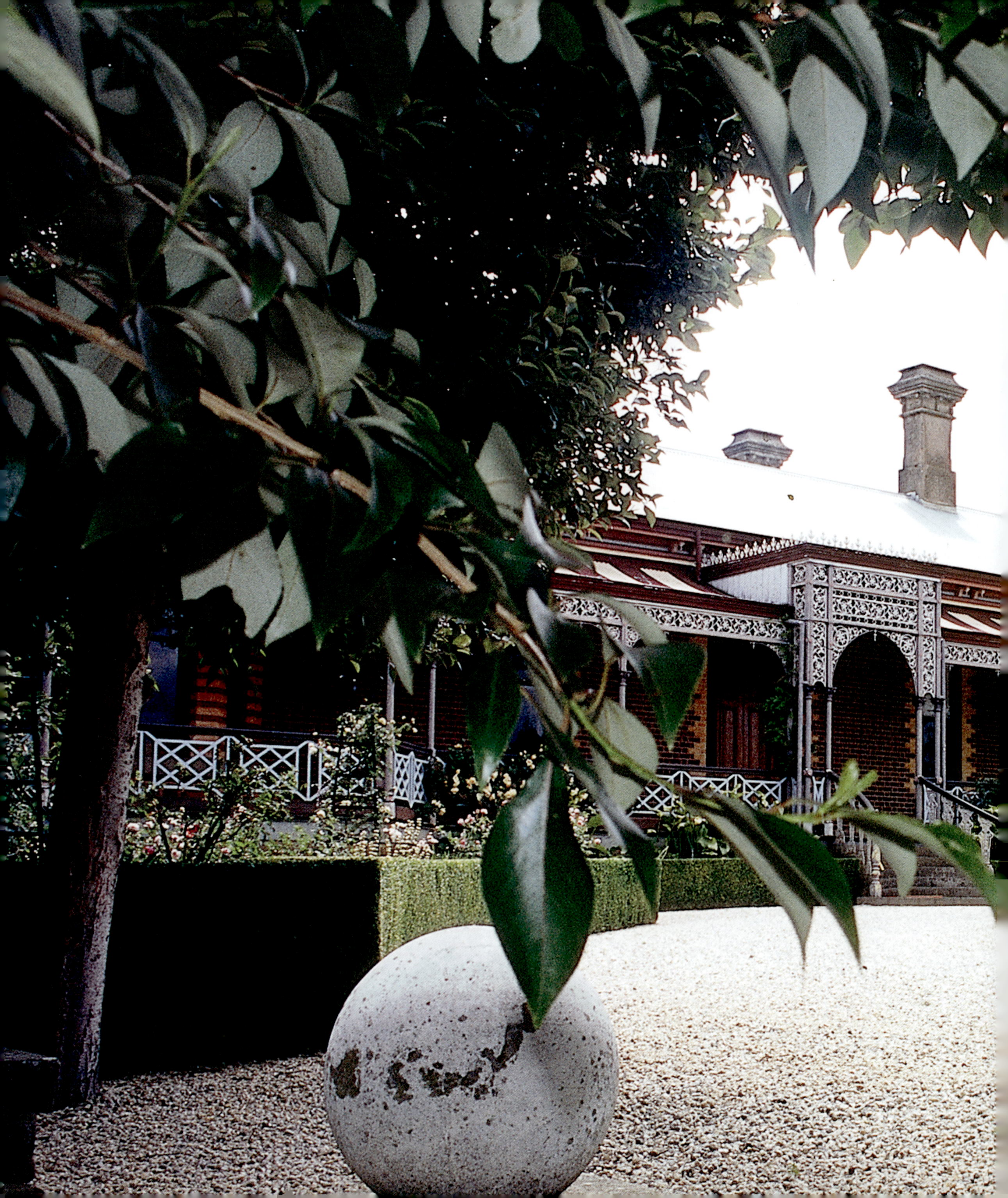

Larundel

Larundel's grand country house is the perfect foil for the classic garden of spectacular proportions that surrounds it

The classical style of garden within the grounds of a country estate has a rich history . Think of places like the Château de Villandry in France, or Sissinghurst in England. But at Larundel, a grand country homestead in Victoria's Western District, the formal garden as we know it has been given a very contemporary twist.

Like the house's interior, which was redecorated by flamboyant Australian designer John Coote, Larundel's exterior is far from ordinary. A whimsical iron bedhead offers light-hearted relief from the formality of the French potager, a planting of artichokes adds humour to the white garden and – when they're allowed to – the spring lambs put on an enchanting performance in the pear walk. It may have been designed by Paul Bangay but this is not your average classical estate.

In essence, Larundel is horticultural opera at its very best: an extraordinary display of greenery, stone and garden 'rooms' punctuated by a sprinkling of reflection pools, parterres and urns that entrances all those priviledged enough to see it.

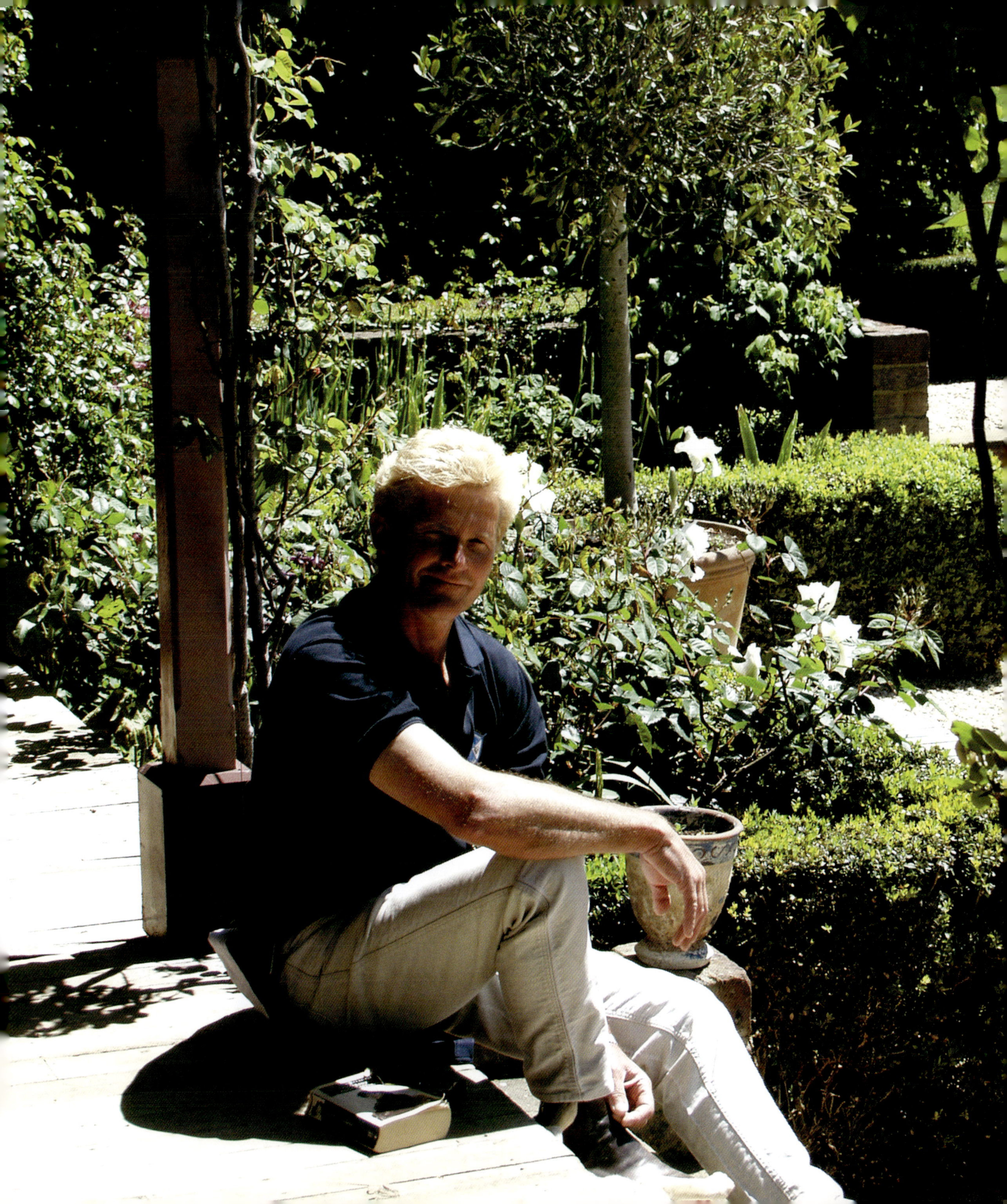

Defined by a perimeter of high hedges and softened by a copse of silver birches, the meditation garden, left, is a perfect place to sit and reflect: a natural punctuation mark in a garden full of beauty and prose.

COUNTRY ESTATES

Views sublime: The vista, far left, over the surrounding countryside is as striking as the rest of the garden, and owners Paul and Gabrielle Preat, left, have plans to take the garden to even more dramatic levels of horticultural theatre.

LARUNDEL

The architectural historian Mark Girouard speaks at great length about the country house in his book *Life in the English Country House*. Country houses, he says, were essentially 'power houses' built to enhance their owners' ability to influence local and national politics. Certainly some of the great houses, especially those in England, were built to impress, with designs that dominated the landscape. Country houses also often served as central places for the ruling class to discuss election campaigns, among other political strategies – not surprising, really, since many of their aristocratic owners and/or members of their families were members of parliament. Nowadays, of course, anyone can own a country house, no matter what your profession. Although it does help if you have a successful business – or at least an understanding bank manager – behind you.

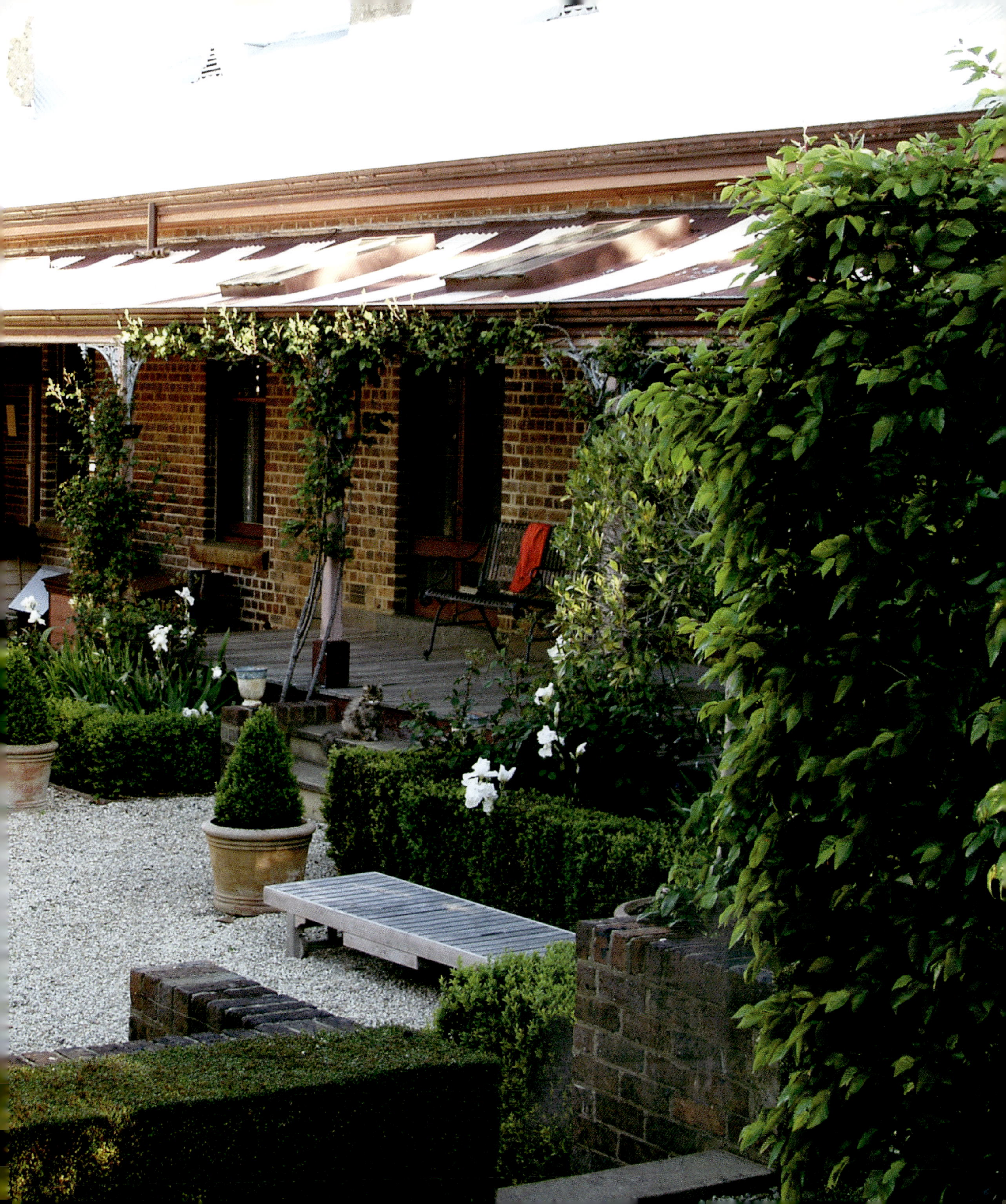

The sense of theatre at Larundel stems from the typical features of a classic garden – the precise angles and symmetrical lines – and landscape designer Paul Bangay's signature style can easily be seen around the property: everything is in its place and in perfect Bangay-esque proportion.

But there are also intervals of cheekiness among the acres of calm, including parterres, birdhouses and gates in surprising places, and the stables, which are painted a delightful shade of porcelain blue – the same delicate shade of blue as the enormous country kitchen.

It is a property that is at once chic and liveable. The spaces may be exhaustingly large (especially when you have to clip, clear or clean them), but each – whether exterior or interior – is filled with objects that carry an imprint of the owners' elegant style, making them visually warm and beautifully inviting. The study (shown next page), which is decorated in a particularly rich shade of country-house red, is filled with remnants of rural living: a pair of well-worn polo boots and gloves, paintings and statuettes of thoroughbreds, and a coffee table fashioned out of old tomes. The main bathroom, meanwhile, is a luxurious but entirely usuable bathing space that's loved by all the family, including two-year-old Will, who happily splashes around in the giant claw-foot tub each night.

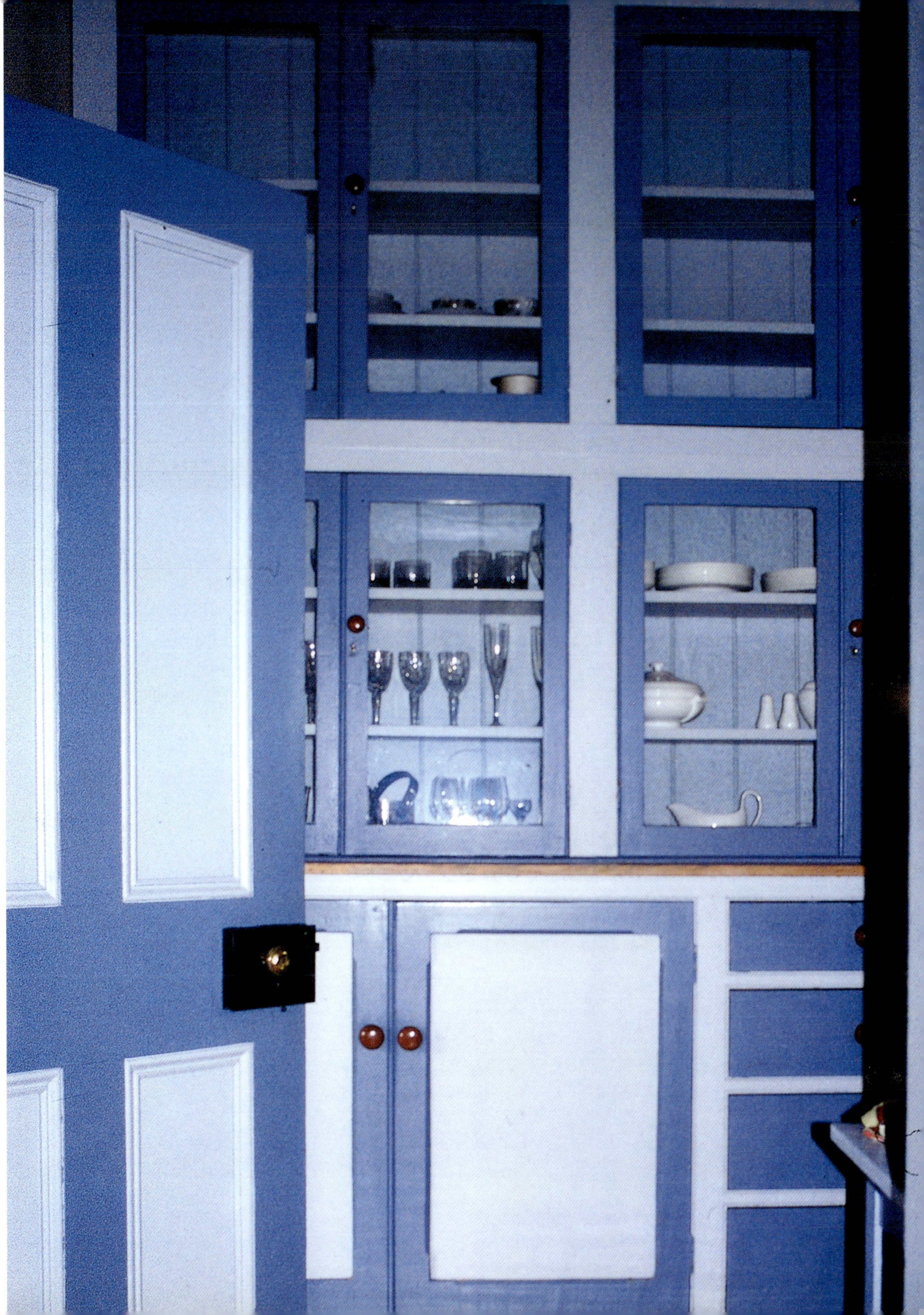

COUNTRY ESTATES

LARUNDEL

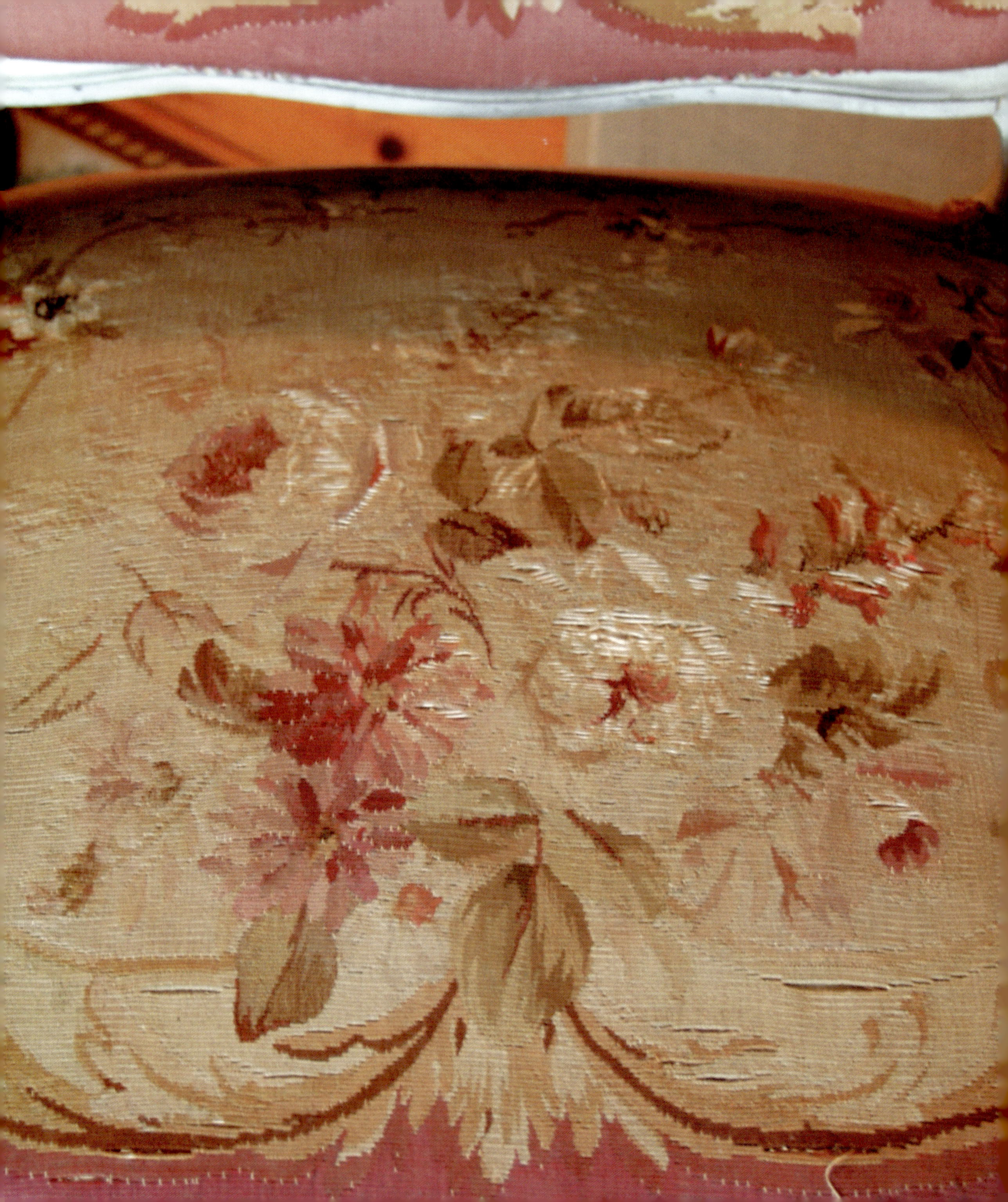

BERRIES AND CREAM CUPS

INGREDIENTS

1 punnett strawberries
1 punnett blueberries
1 punnett raspberries
fresh double cream

Wash blueberries, strawberries and raspberries. Cut the strawberries into halves. Mix together and fill four glasses with equal mixes of all three berries. Top with a generous dollop of double cream. Serve with champagne.

A HEIRARCHY OF COUNTRY HOUSE STAFF (IN A TYPICAL COUNTRY HOUSE)

FEMALE STAFF:

Lady's Maid (upper servant)
Housekeeper (upper servant)
First Housemaid (lower servant)
Second Housemaid (lower servant)
Third Housemaid (lower servant)

MALE STAFF:

Tutor (upper servant)
Butler (upper servant)
First Footman (lower servant)
Second Footman (lower servant)
Hallboy (lower servant)
Groom (lower servant)

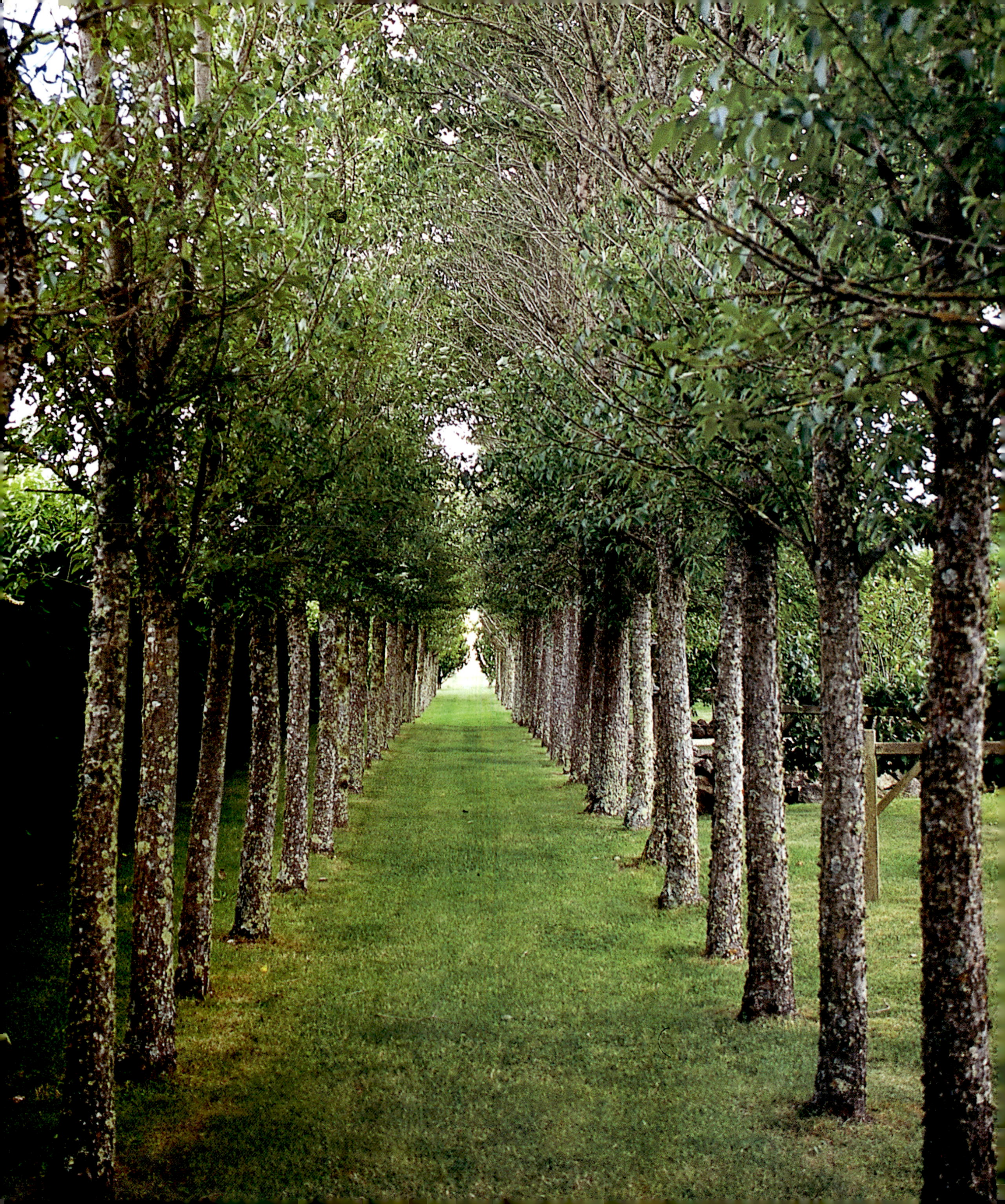

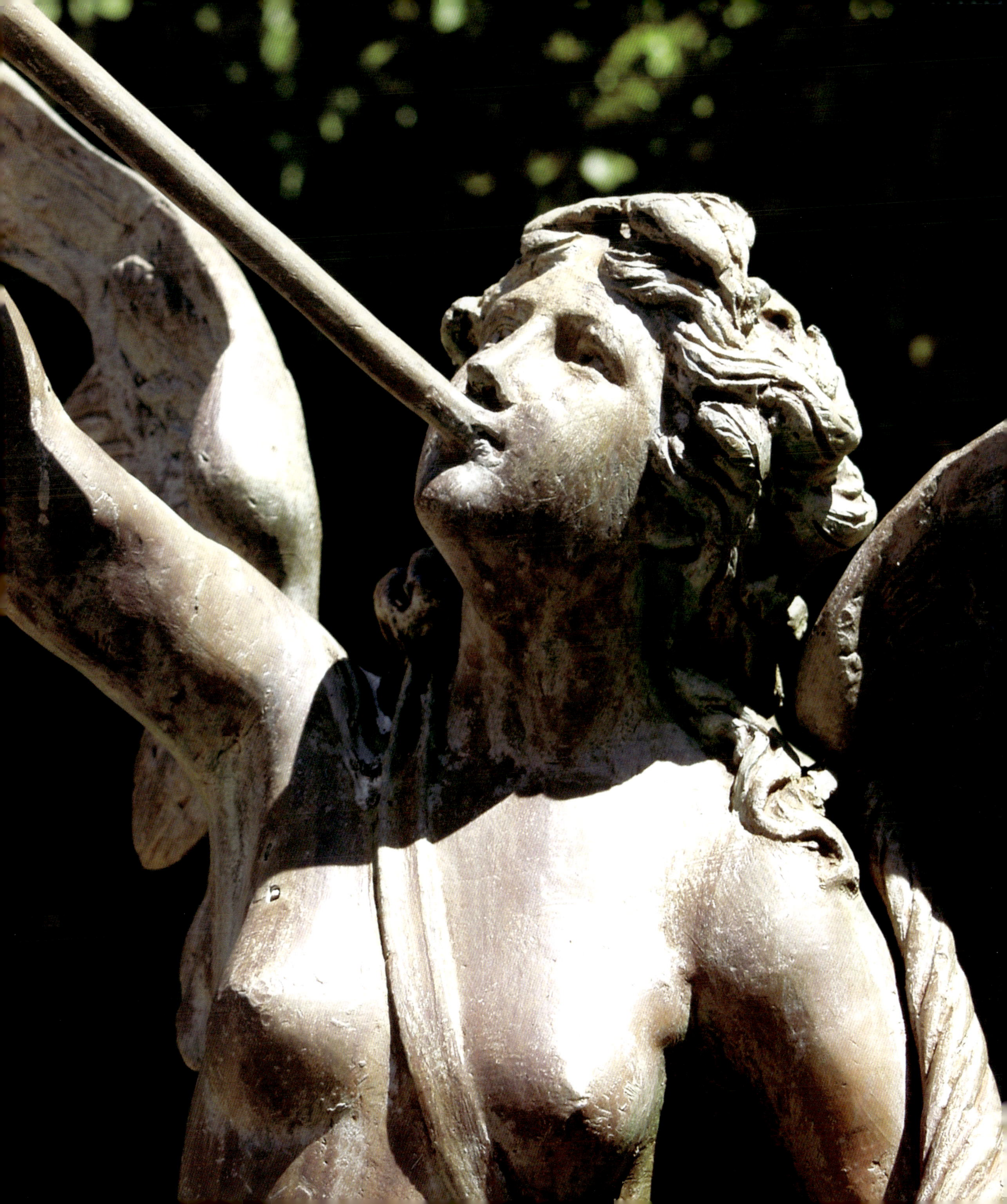

COUNTRY ESTATES

Twenty years in the making, this garden is testament to two extraordinary visionaries: landscape designer Paul Bangay and current owner Paul Preat. The three main components – typical of a classical garden – are outline, symmetry and detail, all of which are elegantly reflected here in the various 'rooms', with their strong axes and sight lines and rich detail.

LARUNDEL

Made up of a series of themed 'rooms' designed on a geometric framework of strong lines and enclosed by immaculately clipped holly hedges, the garden, pictured right, was commissioned more than two decades ago by Larundel's original owner Craig Kimberley, the founder of fashion chain Just Jeans. The preservation of a garden is by its very nature an ephemeral art and rather than remaining static, this is very much a 'garden in motion', with current owners Paul and Gabrielle Preat adding new things almost weekly.

COUNTRY ESTATES

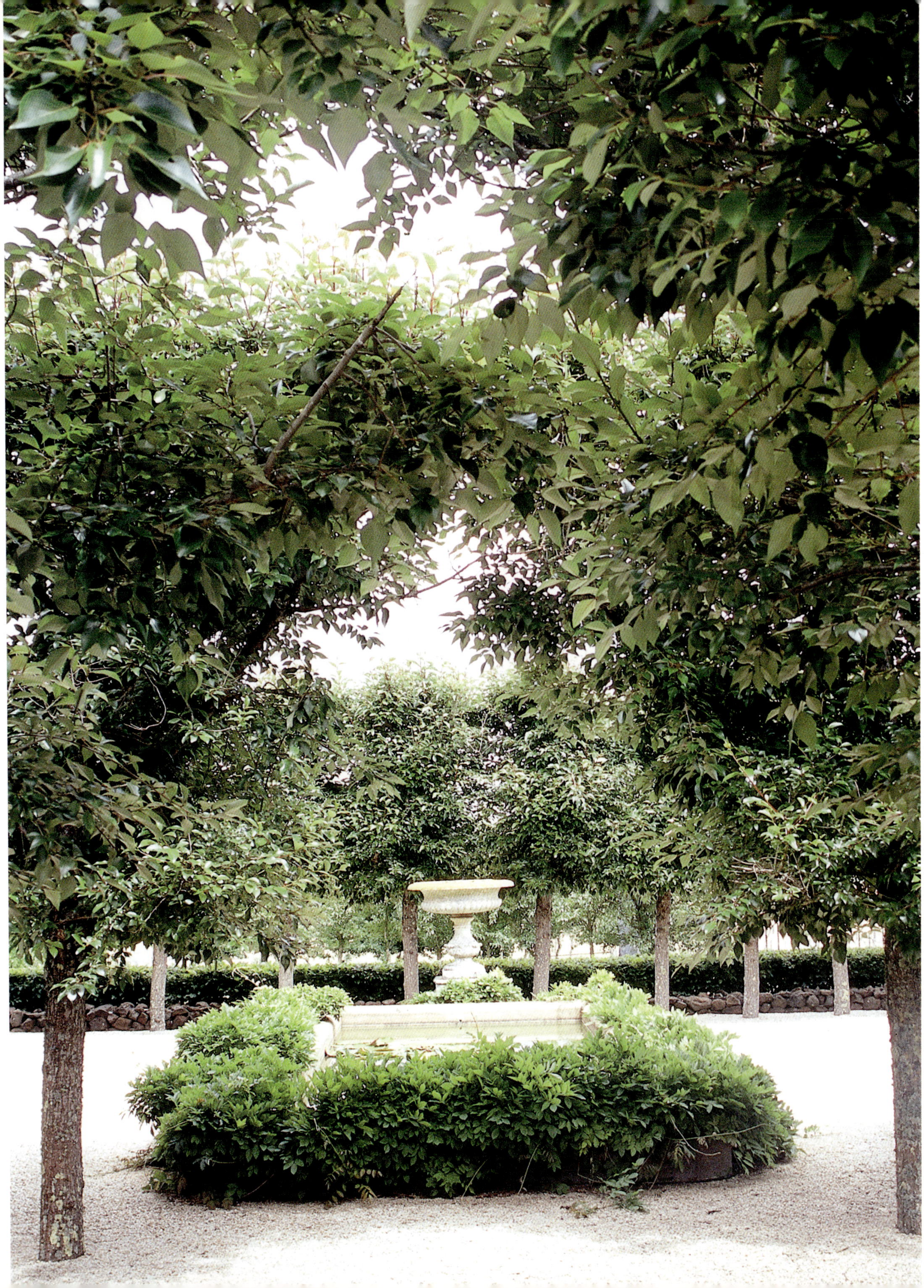

COUNTRY ESTATES

CAVIAR TOASTIES

INGREDIENTS
the best caviar available
crème fraîche
toasties

Spread some crème fraîche on mini toasties, and then top with your favourite caviar. Serve with the Sunday papers and your favourite champagne.

Yandina Station

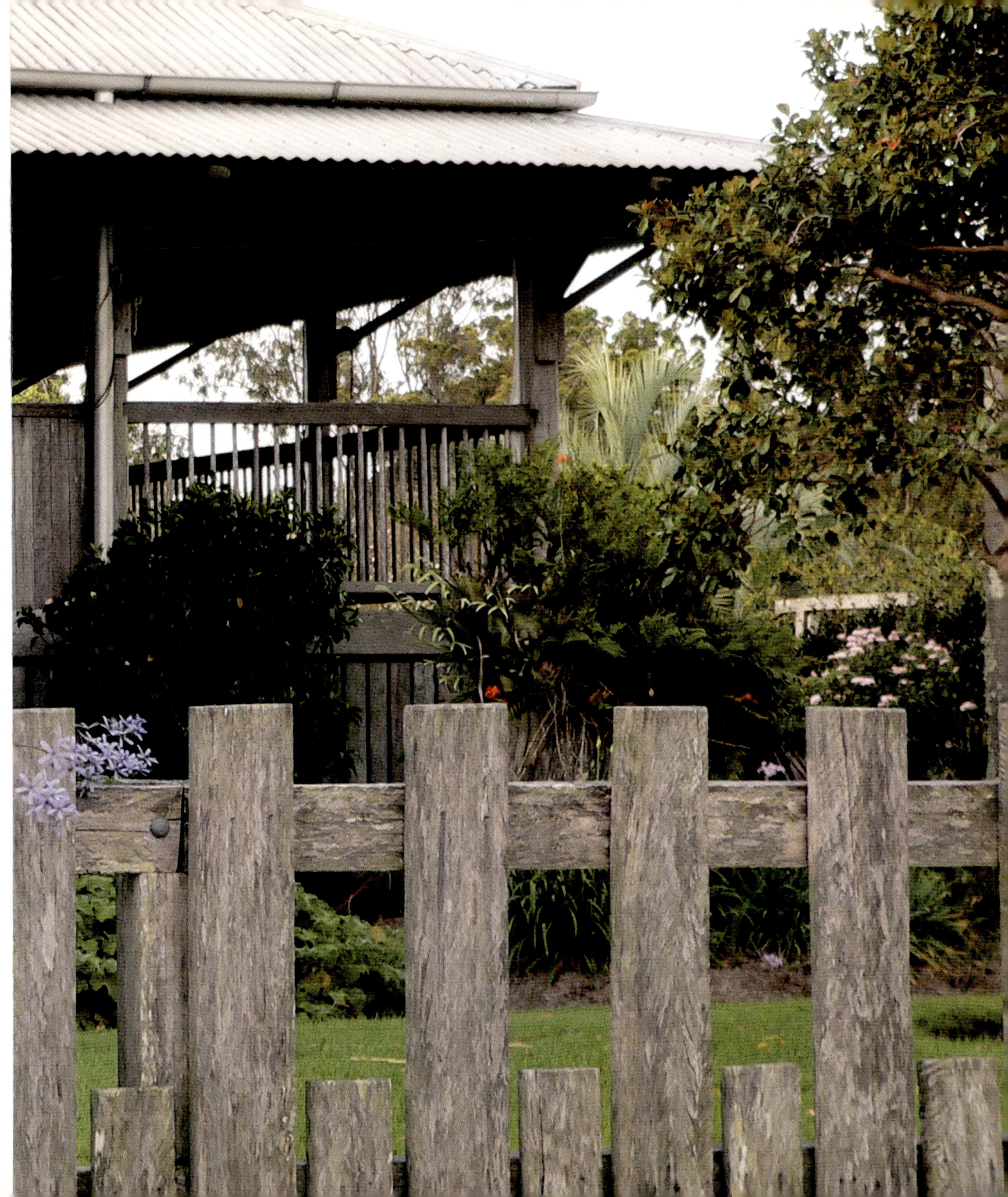

Full of fascinating things, from animals (Brahman cattle, long-necked Indian running ducks, silky hens, woolly sheep), to accessories (including a 1950s grey 'Fergie', or Ferguson, tractor), and farm sheds (including a dairy and sawmill), Yandina Station is an architect's, antique lover's and animal advocate's paradise. The various pieces, whether animal, material or natural (the garden is as fantastic as the rest of the house) are displayed around the place like a gallery of Australiana, and serve as the perfect backdrop for this utterly authentic homestead.

COUNTRY ESTATES

YANDINA STATION 115

The homestead's verandah is the best place to sit and chat with a Bloody Mary as the sun sets over the orchard on a balmy afternoon, while the various corners of the farm make for a sublime spot to set a table and chairs for an elegant luncheon. The station has its own herb and vegetable gardens, and produce is picked daily for the various functions that are often held here. You could say there is a delicious sense of country about it all..

YANDINA STATION 117

Over the years Yandina Station has established a reputation for not only being a gorgeous place but a fabulous space for first class functions. (Sir Richard Branson launched Virgin Blue here when it first started). As a result, Yandina Station's many corners often find themselves being swept out and decorated in readiness for a fabulous soirée. When not entertaining or catering for a crowd, the family like to meander down to one of the two dams for an afternoon picnic – and quite often the animals, including the dogs and sheep, all go too.

COUNTRY ESTATES

Ducks waddle freely around the orchard, farm dogs pitter-patter down pathways, veggies flourish under the water tanks, and a feeling of country productivty pervades the air. As one guest commented, Yandina Station is the original field of dreams.

YANDINA STATION

Food is almost as important to the Schmidt family as farming. In fact, for many years, the property's old dairy was the best place to get a Sunday roast. Yandina Station's main restaurant is still there, in the old homestead, but now only caters to functions and private parties.

COUNTRY ESTATES

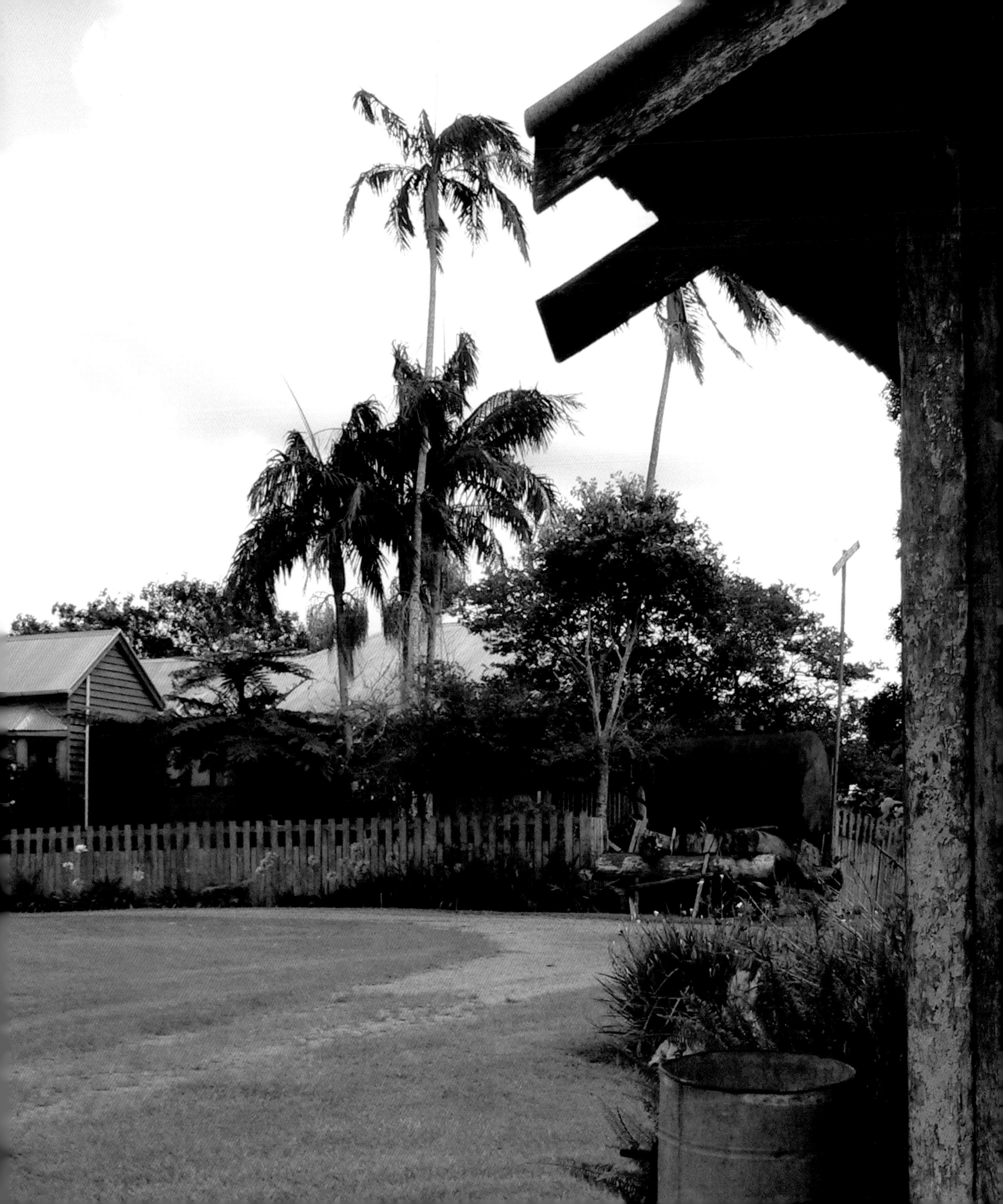

COUNTRY ESTATES

PAN-SEARED EYE FILLET WITH YORKSHIRE PUDDINGS

INGREDIENTS

285ml milk

115g plain flour

pinch salt

3 eggs

vegetable oil

5 large onions

200g of eye fillet per person

Preheat oven to 220C. Mix the ingredients for the Yorkshire pudding batter together. Let rest for 20 minutes in a warm spot. Preheat muffin tin with 1cm of oil in each section in an oven until hot. After the 20 minutes divide the batter into the trays. Cook on top shelf for around 15 to 20 minutes until crisp and puffy.

To make caramelized onions, peel and slice five large onions. Brown them in a pan with olive oil until coloured. Season and add brown sugar and balsamic vinegar to taste. Reduce the liquid if the mix is too runny.

Seal both sides of each piece of beef in a hot pan and finish in the oven to your liking. To make a really good, mix beef stock with red wine and reduce by at least a third. Season to taste. Serve with horseradish mash potato and greens. Enjoy with a glass of good red.

A scattering of vintage farm goods – both inside and outside the homestead – add ambiance and nostalgia to the mise en scene. 'The homestead's interior only took about an hour to decorate!' laughs Sally.

YANDINA STATION

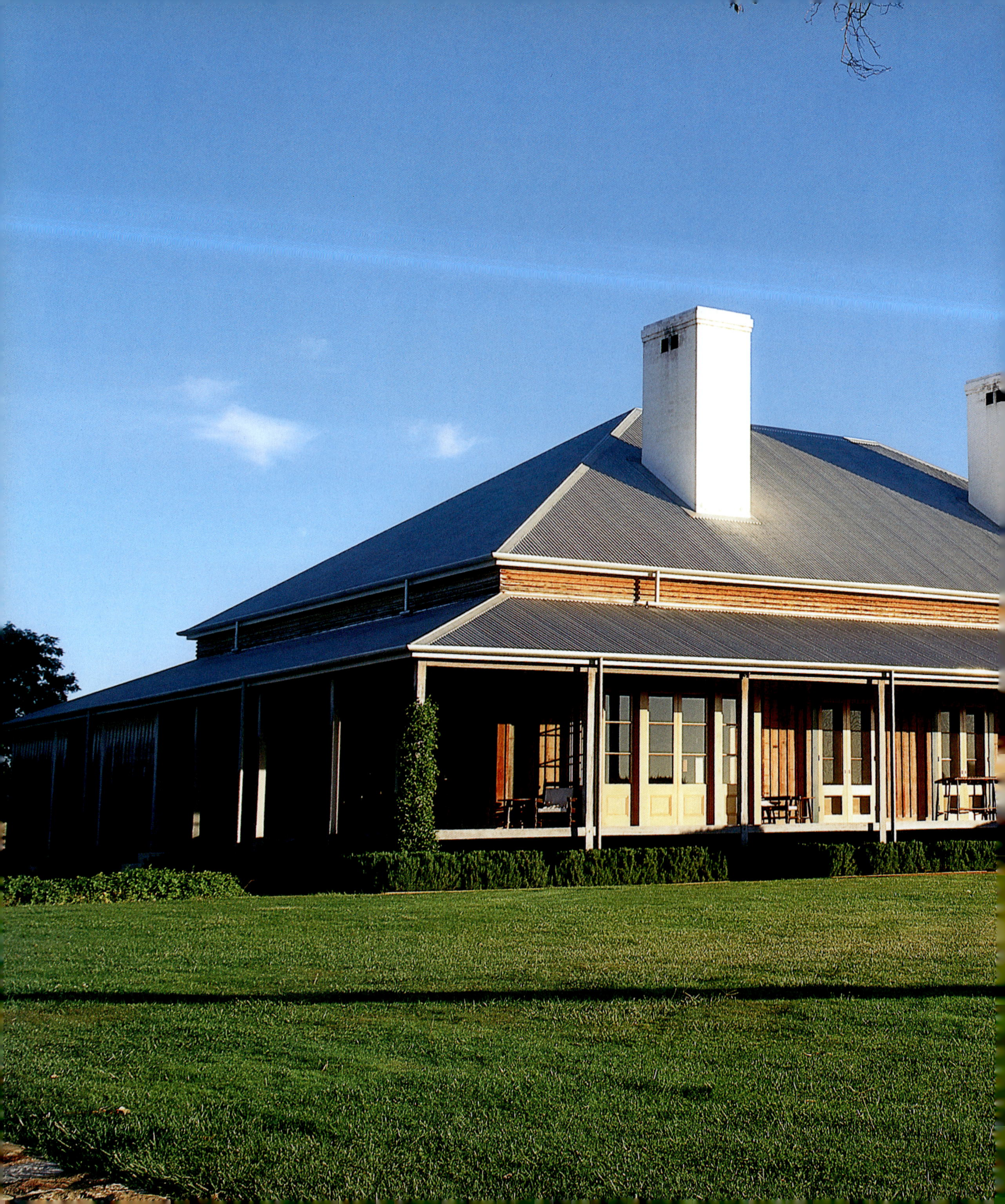

Burrawang West Station

*T*he sky over Burrawang West Station is a quintessential Australian sky: big, blue and tinged with white billowing clouds – a real Henry Lawson sky. It perfectly suits the homestead that lies beneath it, which is something Henry Lawson would also certainly have loved. He would have cherished the landscape too: 10,000 acres of prime cattle country noted for its rich pastures and picturesque scenery.

Here, nestled beneath the big skies and the stoical landscape, dotted with clumps of big old gum trees, there is what could be considered one of Australia's most memorable country experiences, and it's all wrapped up in a traditional homestead that has not only redefined the term 'luxury' but turned country living completely on its head.

Redesigned by leading Melbourne architects Denton Corker Marshall, this grand property, which once encompassed more than 520,000 acres and boasted one of the state's largest

COUNTRY ESTATES

Sweet Pea, who was found on the roadside and raised on the property, is now a permanent feature of Burrawang West homestead.

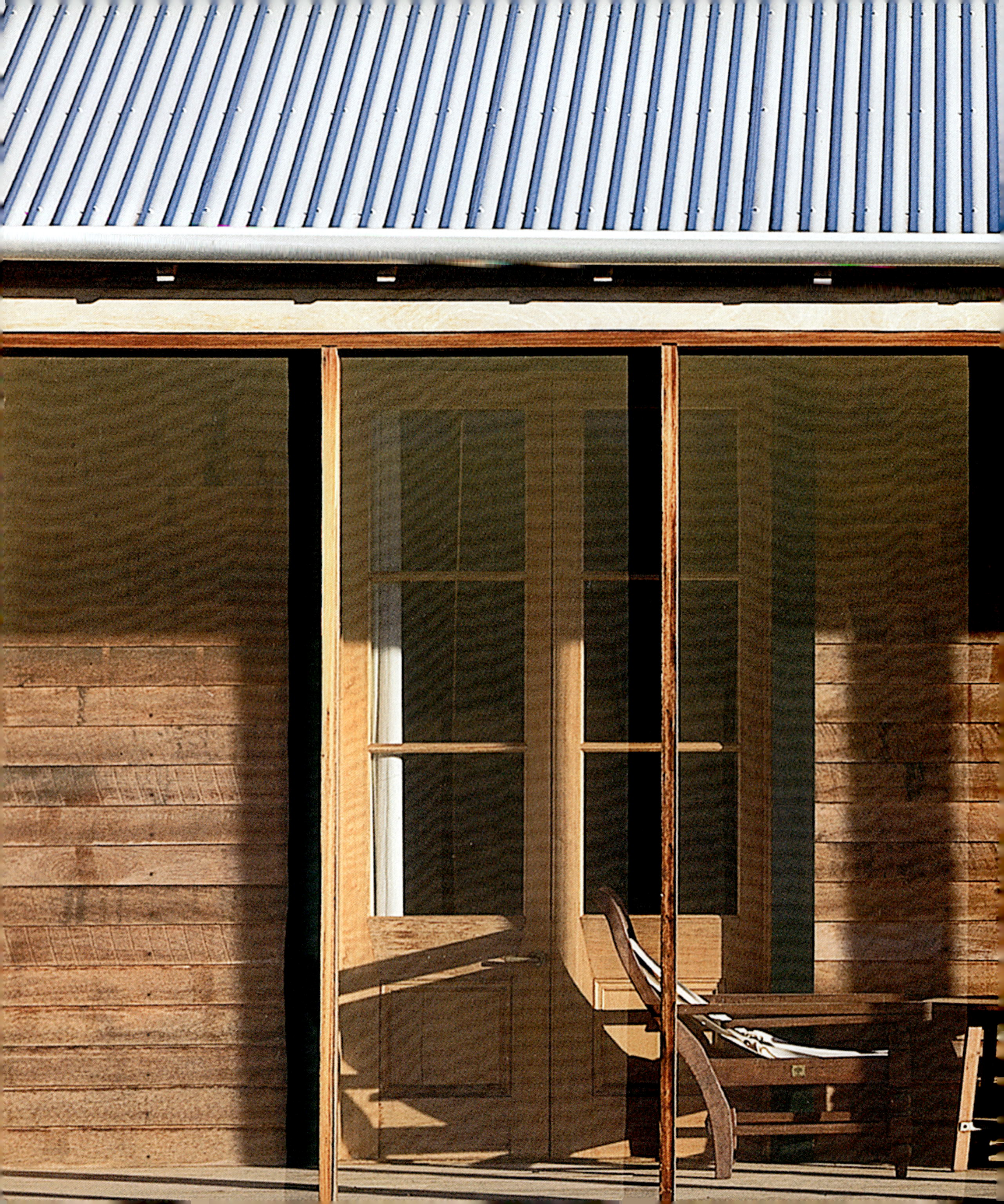

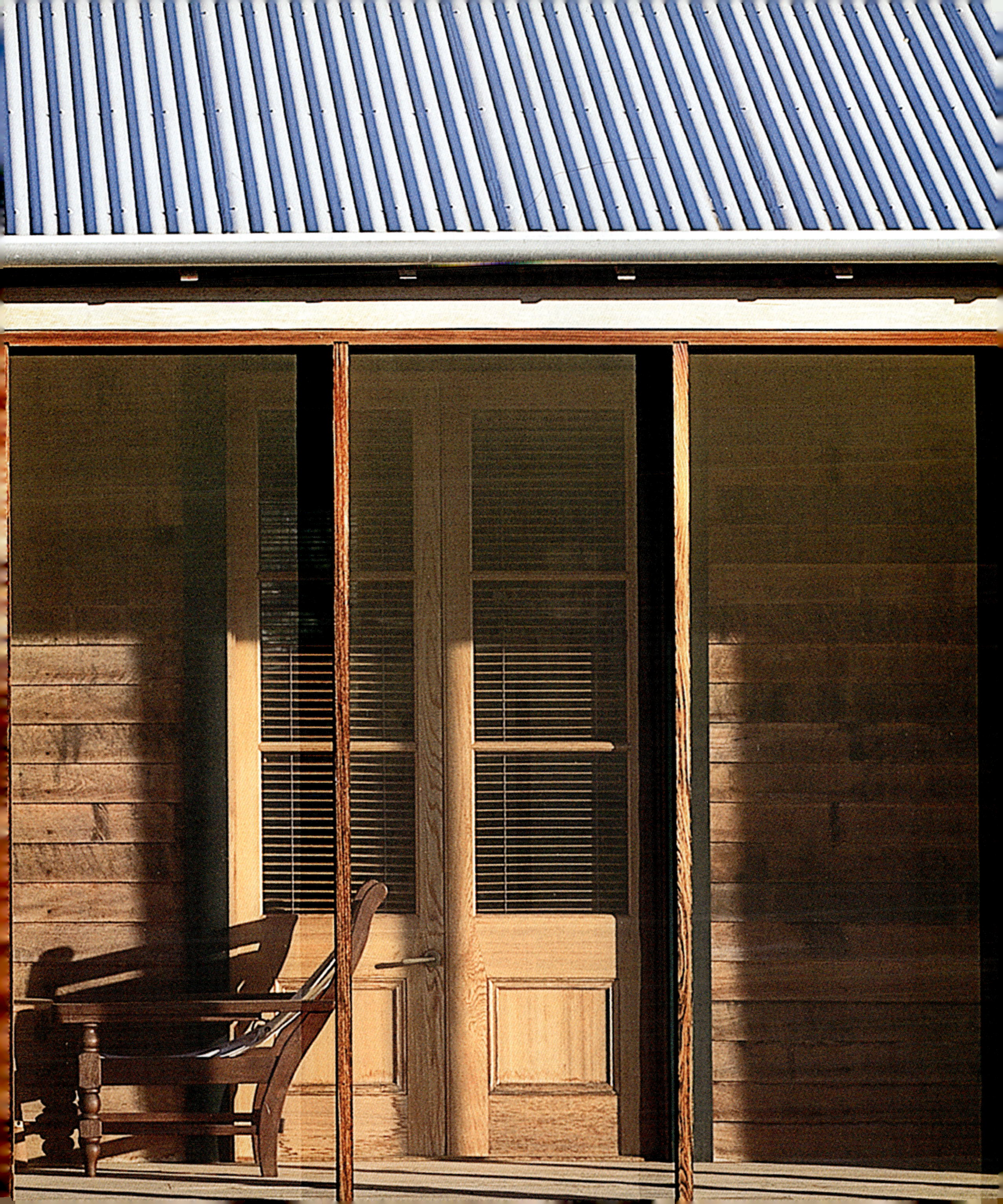

Burrawang West Station has, for various reasons, changed hands several times. It was eventually bought in 2000 by the current owner, an Australian businessman who opened the retreat to the public, put in an airstrip, and re-established the property as a commercial cattle station, now producing the famous Burrawang beef.

shearing sheds – a 101-stand operation that saw more than 250 men working the shears at one time – is now experiencing a new lease of life under its very modern makeover. The striking redesign not only captures the essence of traditional country life, and all its iconic Aussie imagery, but offers a cutting-edge glimpse at the future of rural style. The decision to employ a group of urban architects, a brave one indeed by the former Japanese owner, has paid off handsomely, because Burrawang is now nothing short of five-star fabulous.

There are still classic farm buildings in abundance here, but they are now more Zen-like than anything else, with fiercely simple, almost Amish-esque lines, while the 'Jackaroo' and 'Jillaroo' guest cottages are so beautifully streamlined, it's as if Giorgio Armani himself had trekked out to the bush to stamp his Milanese style on this otherwise typically Australian place.

But that's not to say that everything has been botoxed and modernised to within an inch of its life. In fact, the exterior timbers were – in true Australian fashion – actually left untreated to weather naturally, while certain classic Australian elements, including the verandahs, were retained so that guests could – in true country fashion – check out the 'serenity' while sipping on their Lipton tea.

It is at once utilitarian and beautiful, a lavish, utterly luxurious, utterly Australian hideaway that makes you rethink homestead style, while remembering how wonderful life in the country can be.

COUNTRY ESTATES

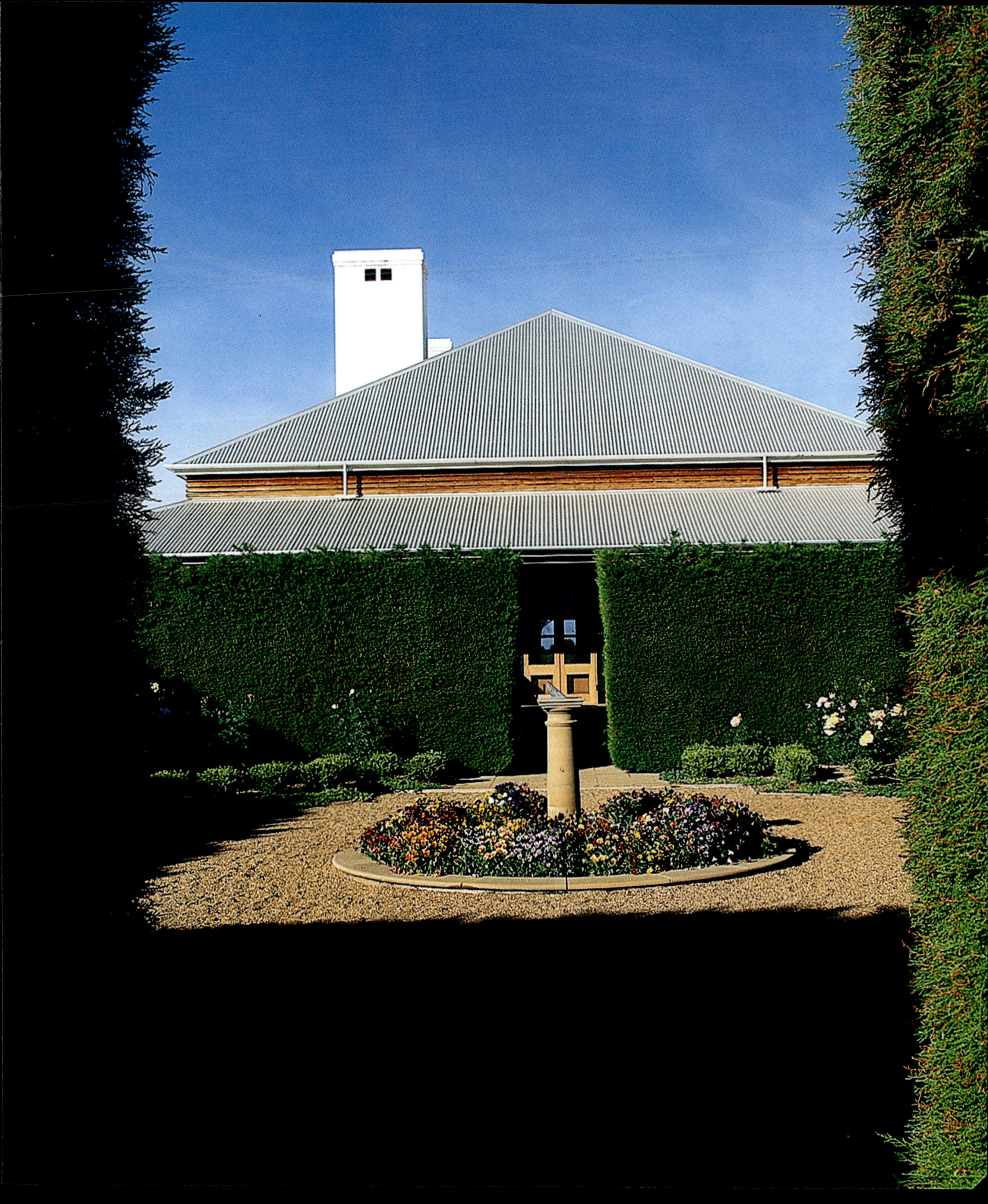

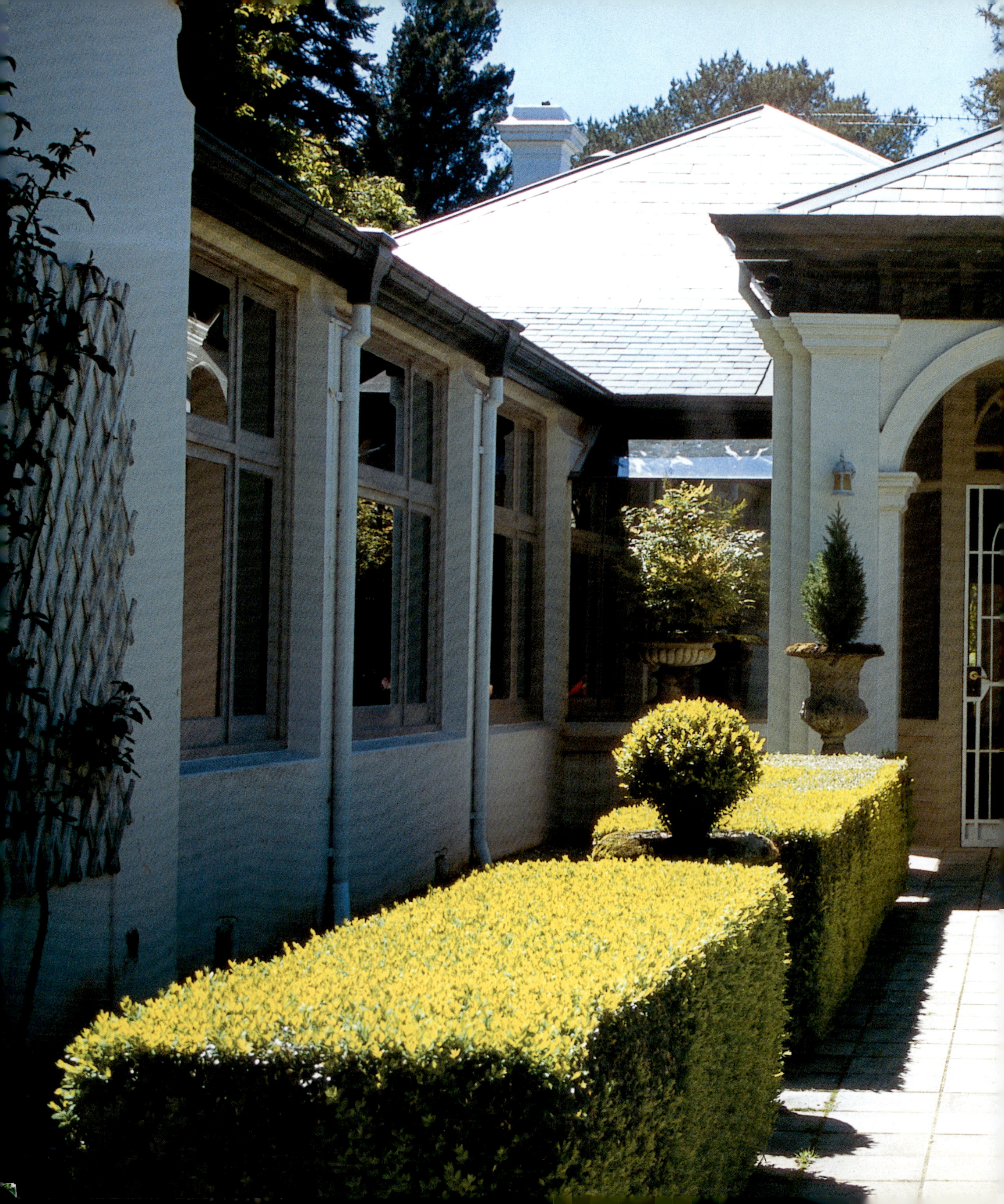

Duneira

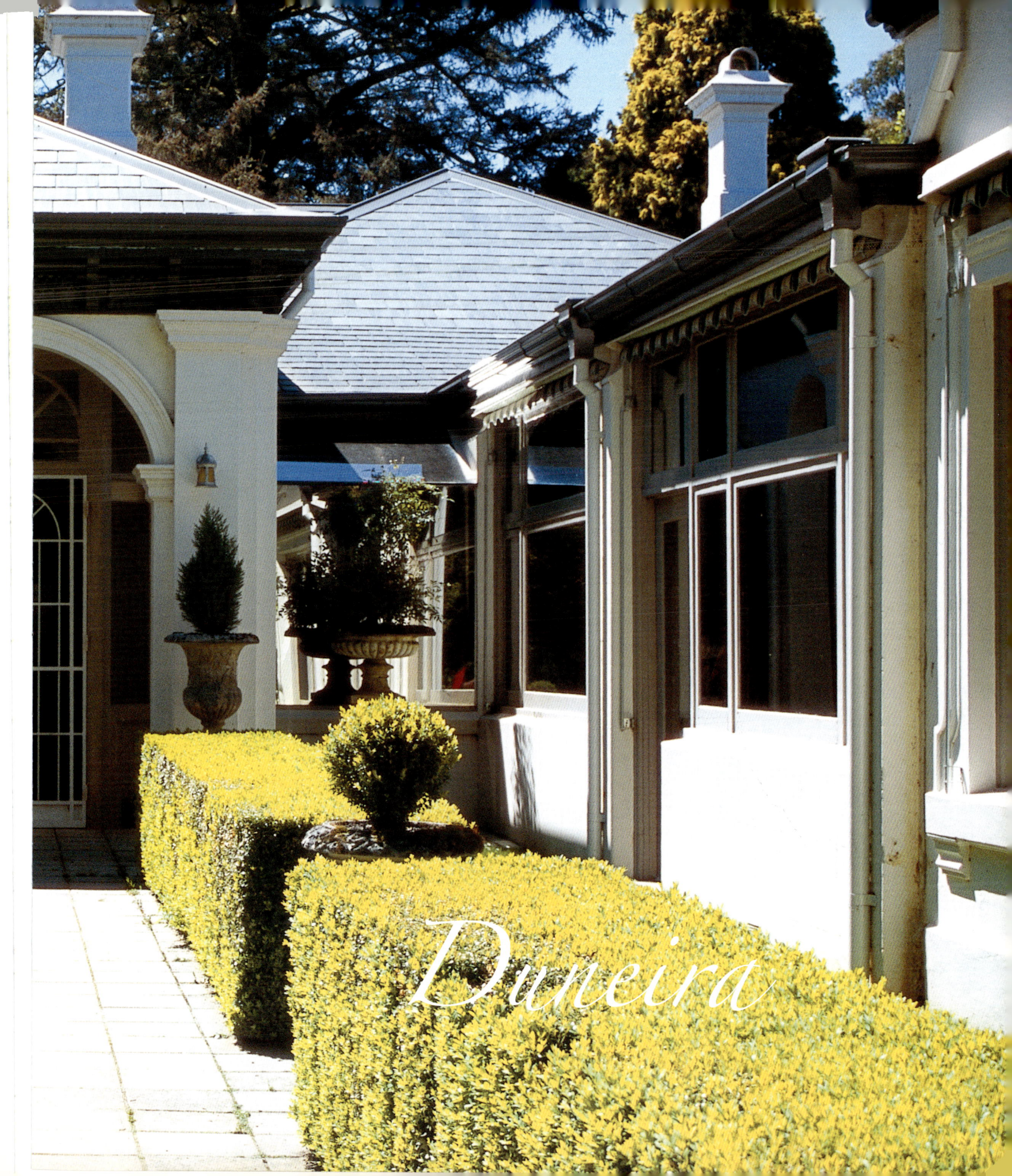

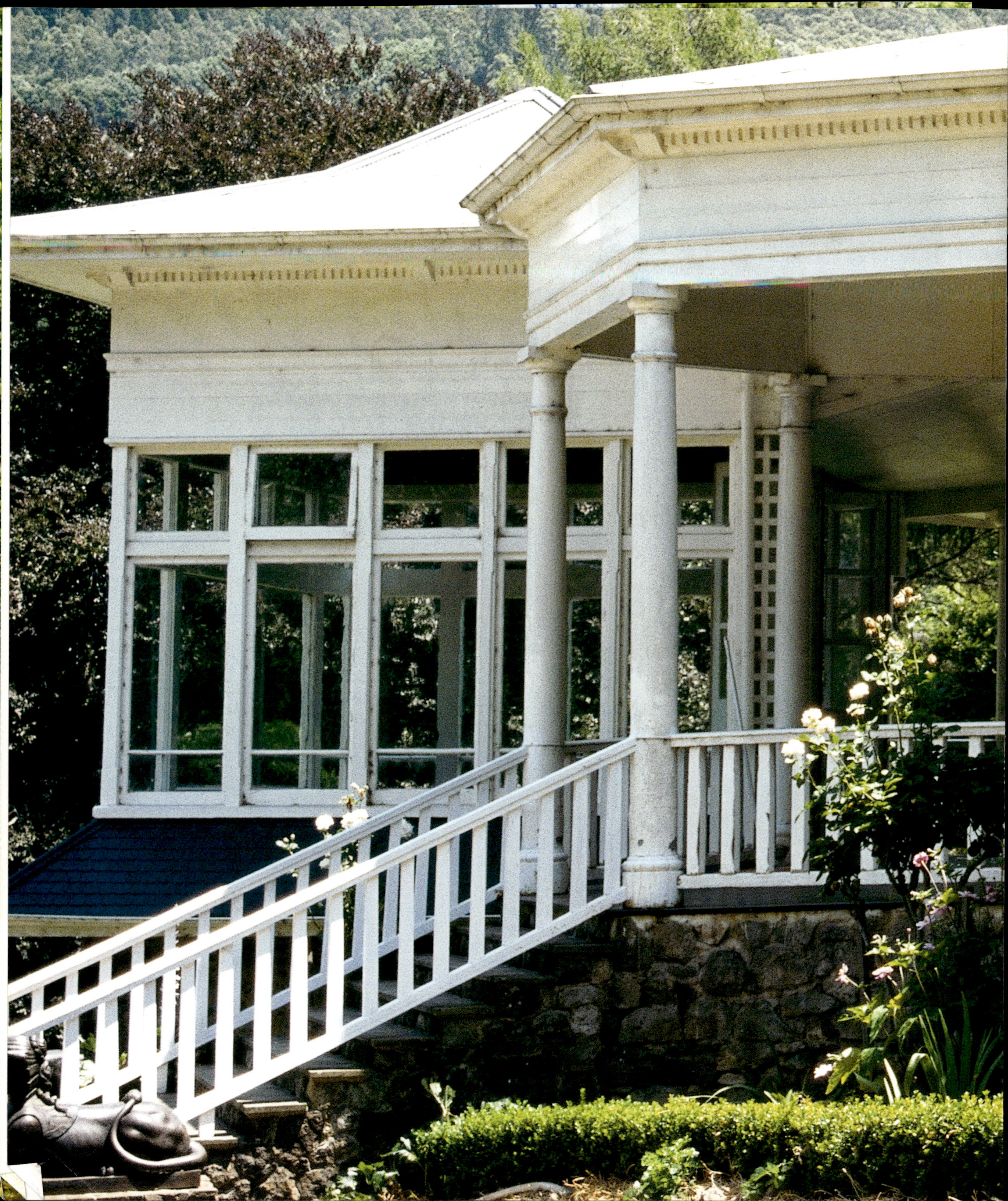

Cameron Lodge

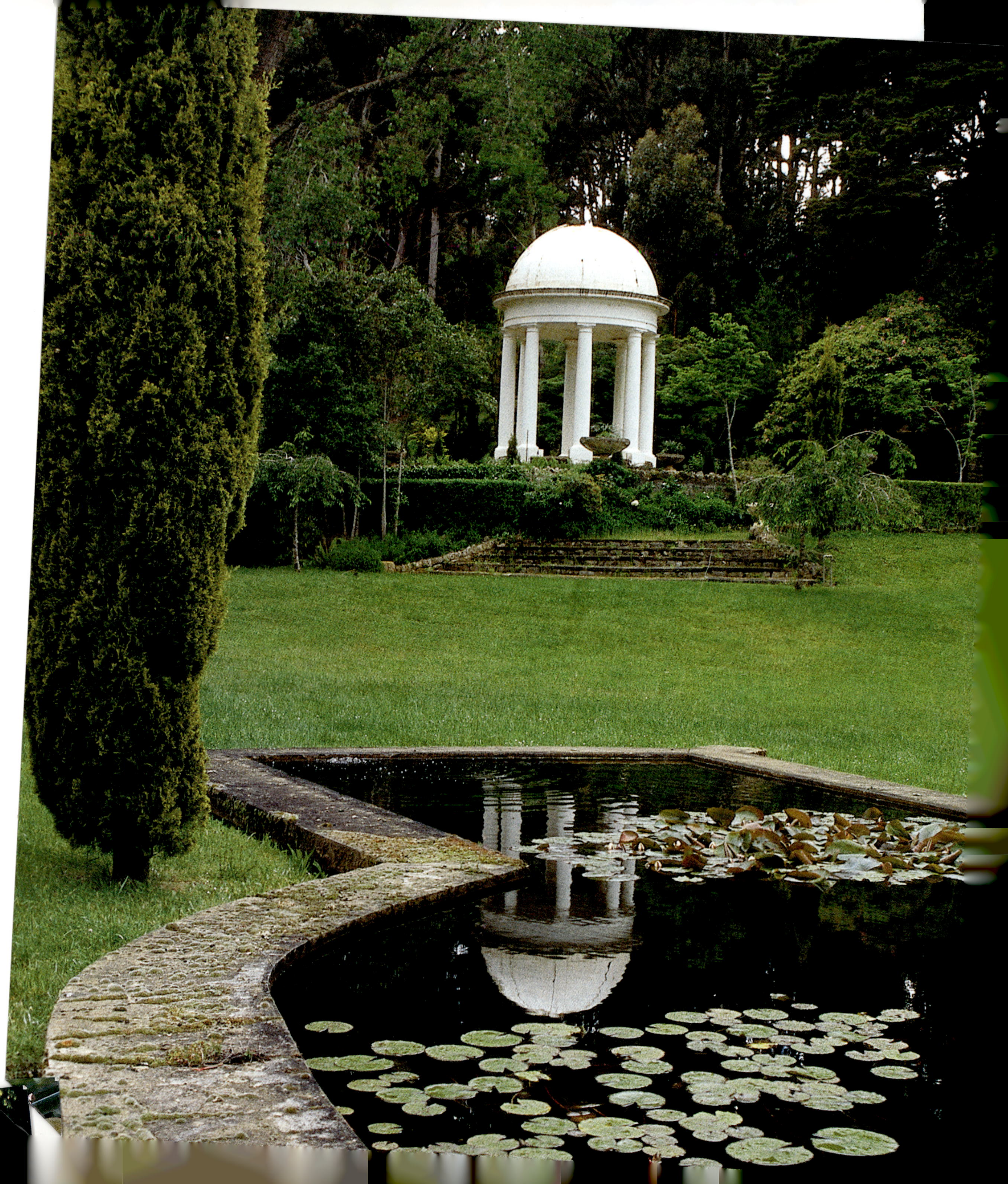

At one end of the estate, there is a handsome tennis court, which is surrounded by stone urns and reached by a magnificent set of wide stone steps. At the other there is an enormous walled kitchen garden. And in between are banks of magnificent hydrangea bushes, a startlingly large fountain, and acres of lawn and mature decidious trees.

At the very bottom of the property, however, is where the highlight really lies.

It is here where the original swimming pool and folly is located, both of which are still intact today. The pool, now used as a pond, was designed in the shape of an old Roman bath and would have almost certainly been the centre for grand soirées in its day. The columned white folly known as The Temple of the Winds, sits on an island surrounded by a moat, and is reached via stone steps shaped like upside-down elephant's feet (a whimsical touch inspired by the Indian hill stations of the sub-continent). There are also four stone elephants in the moat, which spurt jets of water into the air: a magnificent sight on a blazing hot day.

It is a truly impressive country estate, where history, glamour, grandeur and family come together easily as one. As Jane Austen once said, 'if only we all could live in such a place'.

CAMERON LODGE

Country homes and their city counterparts vary in many ways but the one thing many visitors notice most is the way country houses are decorated. Country people very rarely do the 'cut and paste' style of decorating that is so prominent in cities; the textbook look – usually plucked straight from magazines – that dictates you should have a Barcelona chair, a Saarinen table and some Dedede chairs scattered throughout your fiercely minimalist monochrome abode.

In country houses, people tend to follow an 'anything goes' school of design, but ironically, this individual and often whimsical look, in which people are knitted into the place via paintings, heirloom linen and china, pieces of art or sculpture – such as this gorgoeus wire mannequin, above – or merely clusters of hats and boots, can be fiercely chic. It's a mise en scene that's immediately evocative of a life lived well, and epitomises, in many country people's minds at least, true glamour, rather than the ersatz kind.

COUNTRY ESTATES

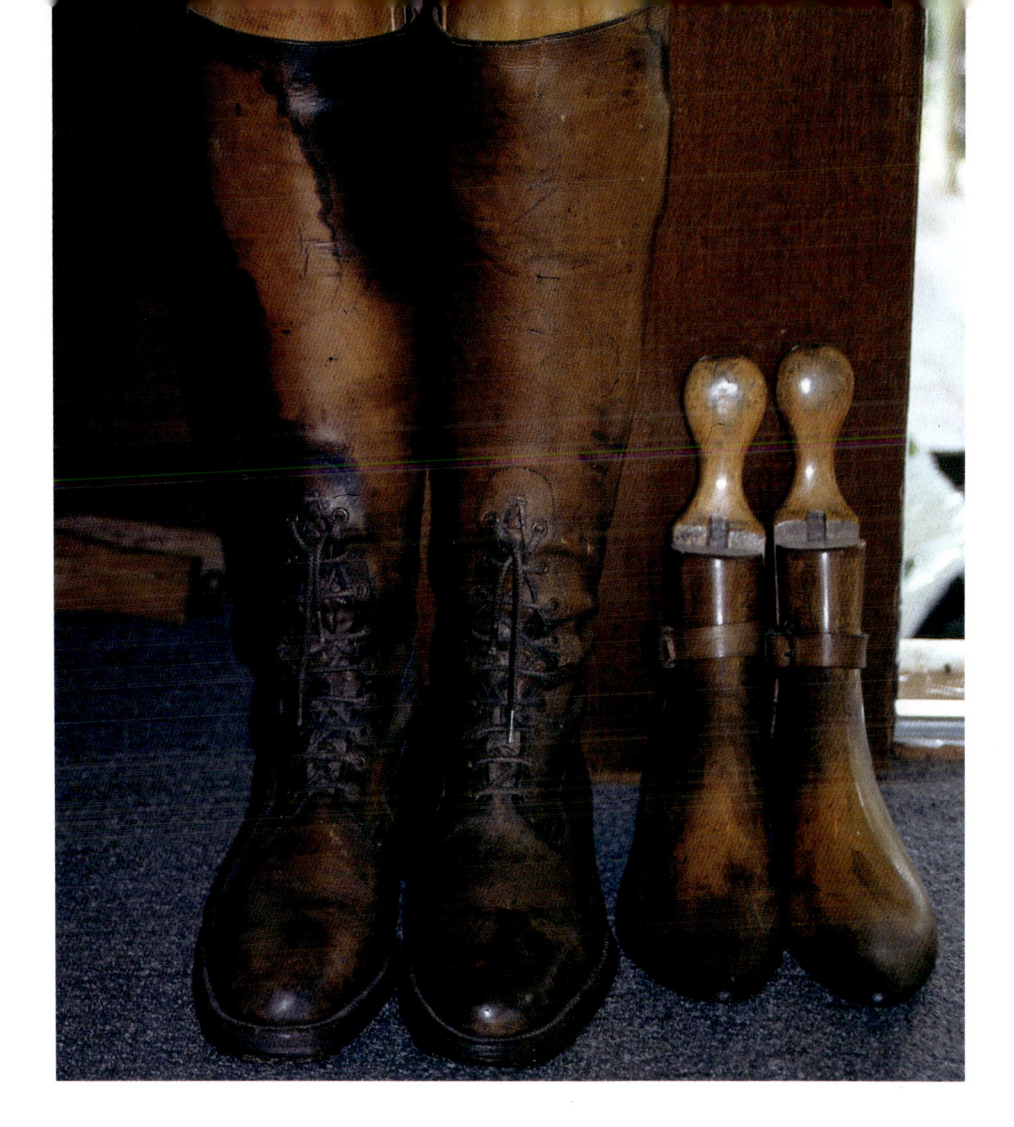

CAMERON LODGE

COUNTRY ESTATES

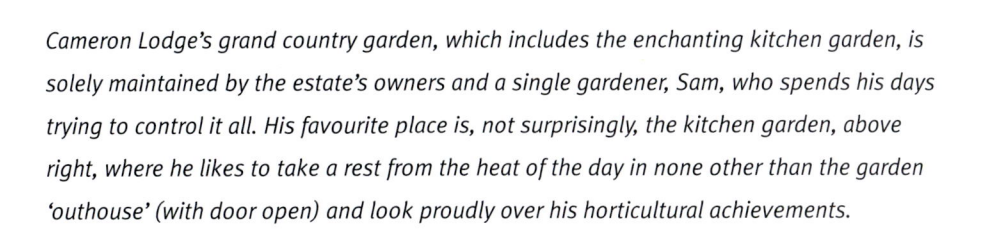

Cameron Lodge's grand country garden, which includes the enchanting kitchen garden, is solely maintained by the estate's owners and a single gardener, Sam, who spends his days trying to control it all. His favourite place is, not surprisingly, the kitchen garden, above right, where he likes to take a rest from the heat of the day in none other than the garden 'outhouse' (with door open) and look proudly over his horticultural achievements.

CAMERON LODGE

Dalvui

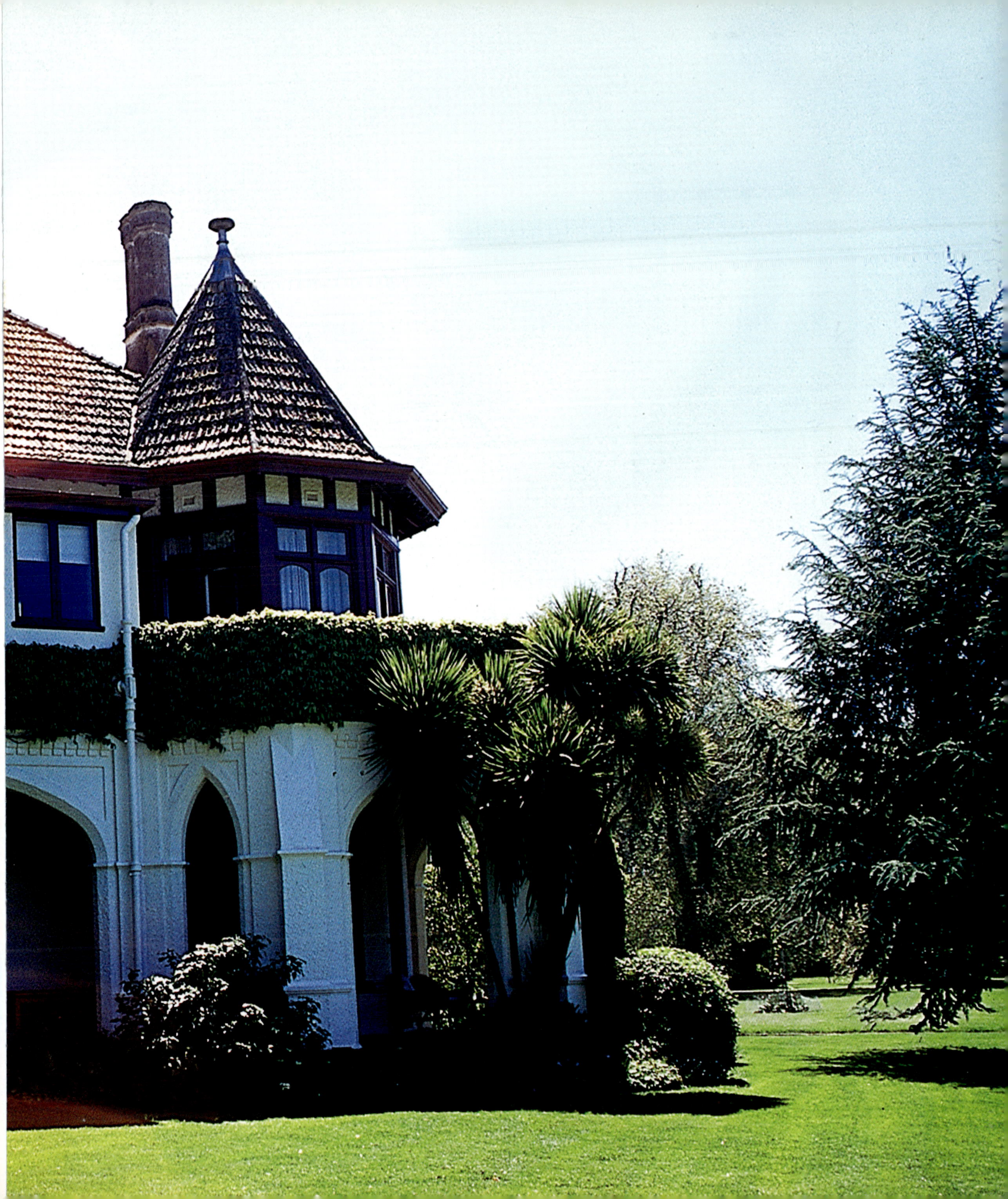

Dalvui's dining room, left, is widely considered one of the most beautiful private dining rooms in Australia, if not the most beautiful, noted for its soaring ceilings, Gothic windows, and of course its sheer size. Neil Black had ordered a beautiful pipe organ for this great space but on his death the family donated it to Geelong Grammar School's chapel. Other highlights of Delvui's 23-room interior include a splendid lift, with a coloured glass roof, which would have been innovative at the time of its installment, a grand entrance hall and staircase lined in Blackwood panelling, many plaster ceilings of Jacobean character, and an inglenook with carved panels by Robert Prenzel.

Cogito ergo sum
EXTREMIS
Libertas
AMICUS MAGIS NE
RIUS QUAM IGNIS
Lupus in fabula

Delvui is still a working farm today, and the various outbuildings include an extraordinarily beautiful stable with clocktower, above, which is now used as a garage. The property's resident chickens meanwhile, provide eggs almost daily as thanks for their free-range existance.

The house was built between 1904 and 1908 by Neil Black, who obtained the land from his father's estate when Neil Black senior died in 1880. Black, a true visionary, immediately commissioned William Guilfoyle to design and plant the garden that would eventually form the estate upon which the homestead stood. The house was then built several years later to a design by Melbourne architects Usher and Kemp. Having completed his home, at the age of 43 years, Black then sailed to Scotland in 1909 to find himself a bride. The ship sank between Durban and Cape Town and no trace of its passengers were ever found. The property was sold to a gentleman, Claude Palmer in 1910, then again in 1984 to Ray Williams, who set about refurbishing the house and gardens, adding 2.5 acres to the grounds. It is now owned by Pam and Peter Habersberger, who have added to the garden yet again.

Dalvui's gardens would have to be some of the most magnificent of any private home in Australia. With the exception of a few minor alterations, such as the removal of the tennis court and the redirection of the driveway, the gardens are thought to conform to the structure imposed in 1898. Highlights include massive rockeries, which Guilfoyle used to mask an outcrop of rock, a sweeping lawn, a lake, a parterre, a 'long walk', a walled garden and garden beds filled with perennials in delicate shades of green, grey and blue.

CLASSIC HEDGEHOG

INGREDIENTS

120g butter

1 egg

1 packet Marie biscuits

1/2 cup sultanas

1/2 cup chopped walnuts

2 tablespoons sugar

1 tablespoon cocoa

Place the biscuits in a bowl and crush with a wooden spoon until they're broken down into rough breadcrumbs. Add sultanas and walnuts. In a saucepan, melt the butter over low heat, then stir in the cocoa and sugar until the sugar is completely dissolved. Add in the lightly beaten egg and stir thoroughly until mixture is smooth. Add the mixture and biscuits together and combine until both are well mixed. Turn into a greased oven-proof dish or lamington tin and press down firmly. Chill overnight in fridge, ice with chocolate icing and sprinkle with chopped waluts. Cut into thick slices the next day. Perfect with a cup of tea.

COUNTRY ESTATES

Delvui's garden covers many acres, and is so impressive it is considered by the National Trust to be of national significance. The essential design, features and planting of Guilfoyle's 1898 design remain remarkably intact, having been carefully maintained by Dalvui's various owners over the years.

The clipped hedges were planted to not only protect the house and garden from prevailing winds but also block out the dry harsh landscape and thus create a little corner of England, which was the aim of many gardens dating from this period. The parterre is a newer addition, and forms a part of the garden that was rejuvenated after the old tennis court was removed. There is also a 'long walk' here, and a birch grove.

Closer to the house there is a walled garden, loved by the chickens, which contains brick pathways that divide beds of roses, bearded irises, and other yellow perennials; an enchanting sight indeed.

There is also a 'pink' garden at the end of the front lawn, which centres around a fabulous silver and pale pink planting scheme.

Ercildoune:

60,000 acres,
24 males,
5 females,
20 horses,
900 cattle,
12,000 sheep.
– Station Diary,
July 4, 1843

40 horses,
3,275 head of cattle,
25,147 sheep.
– Financial statement,
January 1, 1855.

There could be no more evocative name for a country estate than Ercildoune. Just saying it sounds romantic and mysterious, like some grand rambling manor house in an Emily Bronte novel. Fortunately, the reality of this place lives up to the onomatopoeic promise. Ercildoune is everything you imagine it to be: a grand country mansion designed in the vernacular of a baronial Scottish castle that whispers of sentiment and intrigue.

For visitors, the anticipation begins as soon as you start up the driveway and glimpse the mammoth granite mansion stencilled against the sky. The two-storey homestead, which evolved from a single-storey stone house built in the mid-1800s, is one of the finest examples of the Western District pastoral estates of the 19th century. It originally covered more than 60,000 acres, and at one stage was more akin to a small rural settlement than a mere country estate, with the central homestead joined by an array of buildings including a caretaker's residence, a manager's residence, a gatehouse residence and a series of farm sheds such as barns and shearing sheds. It even had its own school and jail.

Present owners John and Christine Dever saw it advertised for sale while down on the Mornington Peninsula in 1999 and confessed to falling in love with it at once: its romantic façade – with its gabled roofs and crow-stepped and castellated parapets – its past, and its potential. If the country house is a great historian then Ercildoune

COUNTRY ESTATES

is certainly an anthology of fabulous stories. Dame Nellie Melba once leased the entire estate for six months in 1907, just after she had finished doing *La Boheme*. Melba had contracted bronchial pneumonia and recuperated at Ercildoune, ordering a hard surface tennis court to be constructed overlooking the front lake (there was already a grass tennis court and croquet lawn), and filling the place with guests.

When they came to live on the estate, however, the Devers shouldered the difficult task of preserving the place. The house had been neglected and the interior was a crumbling mess, painted with possum and sheep droppings. But, thanks to Christine's innate style and John's muscular enthusiasm, the house was slowly renovated, granite block by granite block. The Devers were sensitive enough – and knowledgeable about Heritage and National Trust listings – to leave the 'bones' of the house intact, including most of the original rooms, such as the meat-safe, bakehouse, laundry, wash house, extensive kitchens and servants' quarters, and simply upgraded the interior. With the help of interior decorator Dianne Gow and an army of painters, carpenters, plasterers, tilers and electricians, the old house slowly came to life again.

Ercildoune's estate was once so big, it comprised its own self-sufficient settlement. Mornings were announced by the sound of a bell outside the stable complex, which was run six mornings of the week at 6.45AM. If the men weren't assembled around this bell by 6.55AM to get their day's orders, they lost that day's work and wages. The servant's bell system is still in place, and can be seen in the servant's entrance. In 1841, the number of staff required to look after the place numbered 39 (35 men and four women). At the height of Sir Samuel Wilson's residency, there were 125 on staff. Today there are just three.

ERCILDOUNE

The Devers were also intrepid in tracking down pieces of furniture that perfectly matched the architecture and mood of the place, since – unlike with some country house purchases – there was virtually nothing in the house when they bought it, except a claw bath and a huge old cast iron oven.

Now, the great rooms are no longer silent. Instead they echo with the sounds of guests and family. Oh, and the occasional ghost. You see, Ercildoune is full of people who love the place so much they've never left. Some have seen an older lady, and others have felt a childlike presence, including a builder who saw the spirit of a little girl get into his ute, where she proceeded to sit with him as he drove nervously down the drive. A former housekeeper also used to see the impression of someone sitting on her bed, even though there was no one in the room with her. She would also come out and see the cushions on the rocking chair arranged as if someone had been sitting there during the night. And two small children once asked who the 'silver people on the stairs' were.

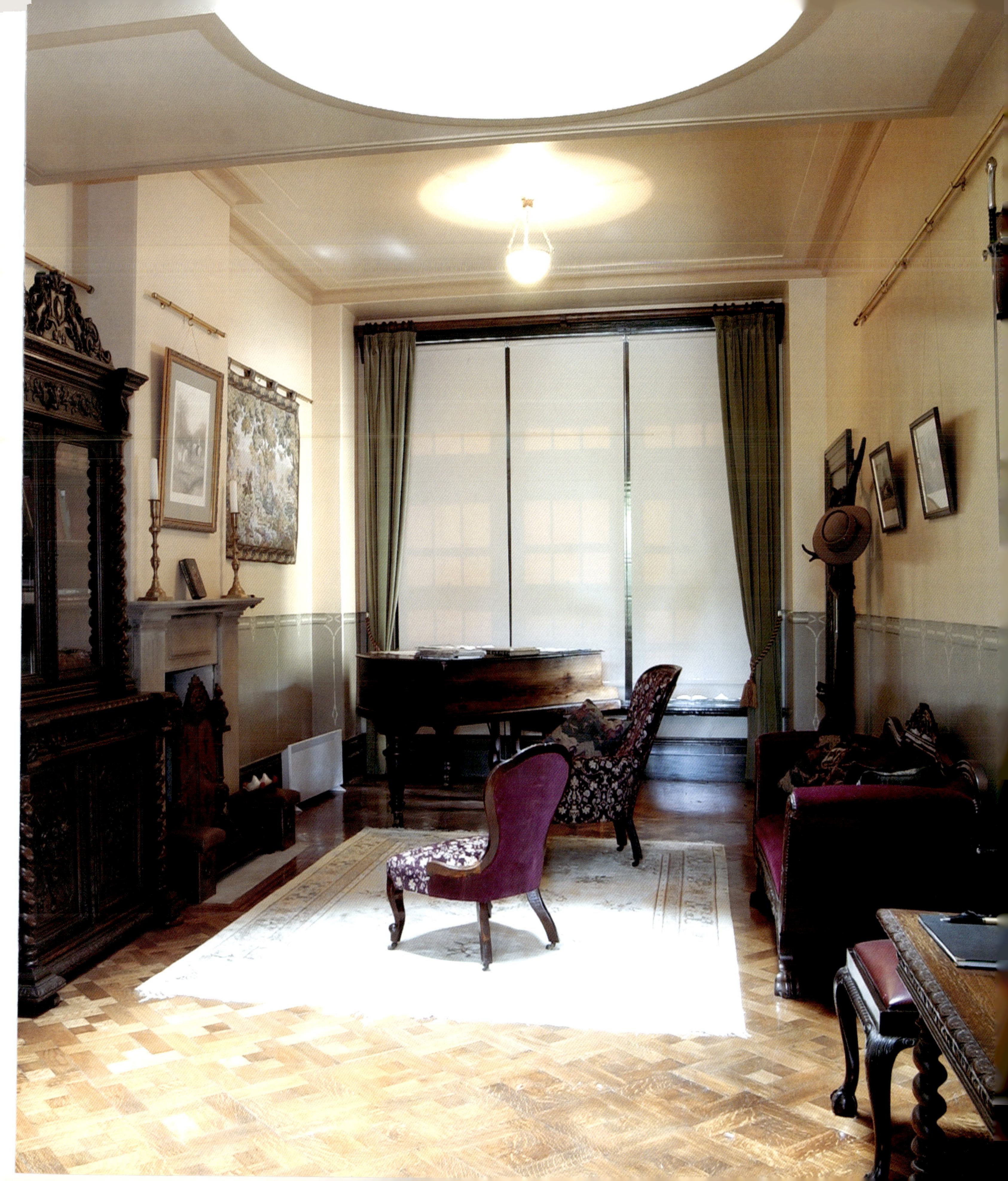

One of the greatest luxuries any country property can have is a walled garden and Ercildoune's is an extraordinary one acre-sized oasis, full of balance and harmony, romance and beauty. Surrounded by an enormous nine-foot granite wall and once filled with enormous hedges that hid the true elegance of these stone surrounds. John and Christine Dever have trimmed the hedges and started again, planting borders of perennials and commissioning an iron arbor reminiscent of those in Melbourne's Botanic Gardens. The difference with this arbor, however, is it's about fifty times the size of its city counterparts. The craftsman, mistaking John Dever's request – or perhaps choosing to diplomatically ignore it – designed a structure that runs almost the length and breadth of the interior, and while some joke that it is as large as a cattle yard, it is far, far more beautiful. The colour and texture of the iron beautifully complements the natural pattern of the stone wall, and when the roses start to climb over the top it will truly be an enchanting place to take a summer stroll away from the heat of the country day.

The garden is one of the oldest in the State, with weeping willows planted as early as 1842. It is also one of the grandest, and most elaborate. Many of the trees were brought over from Scotland and at one stage the entire garden covered nearly 40 acres and encompassed kitchen gardens (everything from potatoes to vines and tobacco), flower gardens and of course the great walled garden. At one stage, there were 13 gardeners employed just to tend to it all. Photographs of Ercildoune taken in 1859 show an

COUNTRY ESTATES

extraordinary landscaping plan, with highly cultivated garden beds, clipped hedges, an ornamental lake, an orchard to the left of the house, many weeping willows and an intricate network of pathways criss-crossing the property. There was also a formal box parterre situated outside the walled garden, which has been sadly lost.

A curvilinear conservatory also dominated a section of the garden, according to records, but has since been destroyed. Other main elements of the original garden that have been lost or abandoned include two orchards, one to the west of the house and the other to the east, and two vegetables gardens, one cultivated by a Chinese gardener to the west of the gatehouse for the larger, field-grown vegetable, and the other to the west of the main house for the smaller table vegetables.

According to writer Peter Watts in *Historic Gardens of Victoria*, there are many clues as to the scale and complexity of this once-grand place: the form of the garden, for one, and the 'shadows' of planting schemes and buildings that still show through. Watts believes it's essential that records, however vague, remain of gardens such as this, so that if they are eventually lost, their plants and design will still be known.

The Devers are following his advice and endeavouring to return Ercildoune's grounds to their former magnificence, battling with nature and the elements, including grasshopper plagues, rabbits and of course resident snakes, as they do so.

Ercildoune's original house was the modest two-storey shelter, below, built in 1837, which still stands today. The upper level was the bedroom and the ground floor a living area built from stone. The house was designed as such to ensure its inhabitants were secure from the local aborigines and bushrangers.

In the 21st century, the term 'country house ' has come to mean everything from a grand estate to a modest cottage. The original meaning for the term, however, was a large house built on an agricultural estate; an estate sizeable enough to enable the landowner to not only live on the income but use it to leverage himself into position as a member of either the aristocracy (the heredity ruling class) or the gentry. The house itself had to be a) enormous, with at least 25 rooms and 8,000 square feet of floorspace, and b) filled to its nine foot-ceilings with antiquities and treasures collected from grand tours around the globe. It also had to have a name, although whether the second word was 'hall', 'castle', 'park', 'palace', 'court', 'abbey', 'priory', or 'grange' depended on both its history and the whim of its owner. If the owner owned more than one country house, and was inclined to travel from one to the other, indulging in pheasant and fox shooting at one, horse racing at another and summer soirées at the third, much of the staff would have to go too. It was an expensive, but obligatory, way of life. Especially if one wanted to succeed in society.

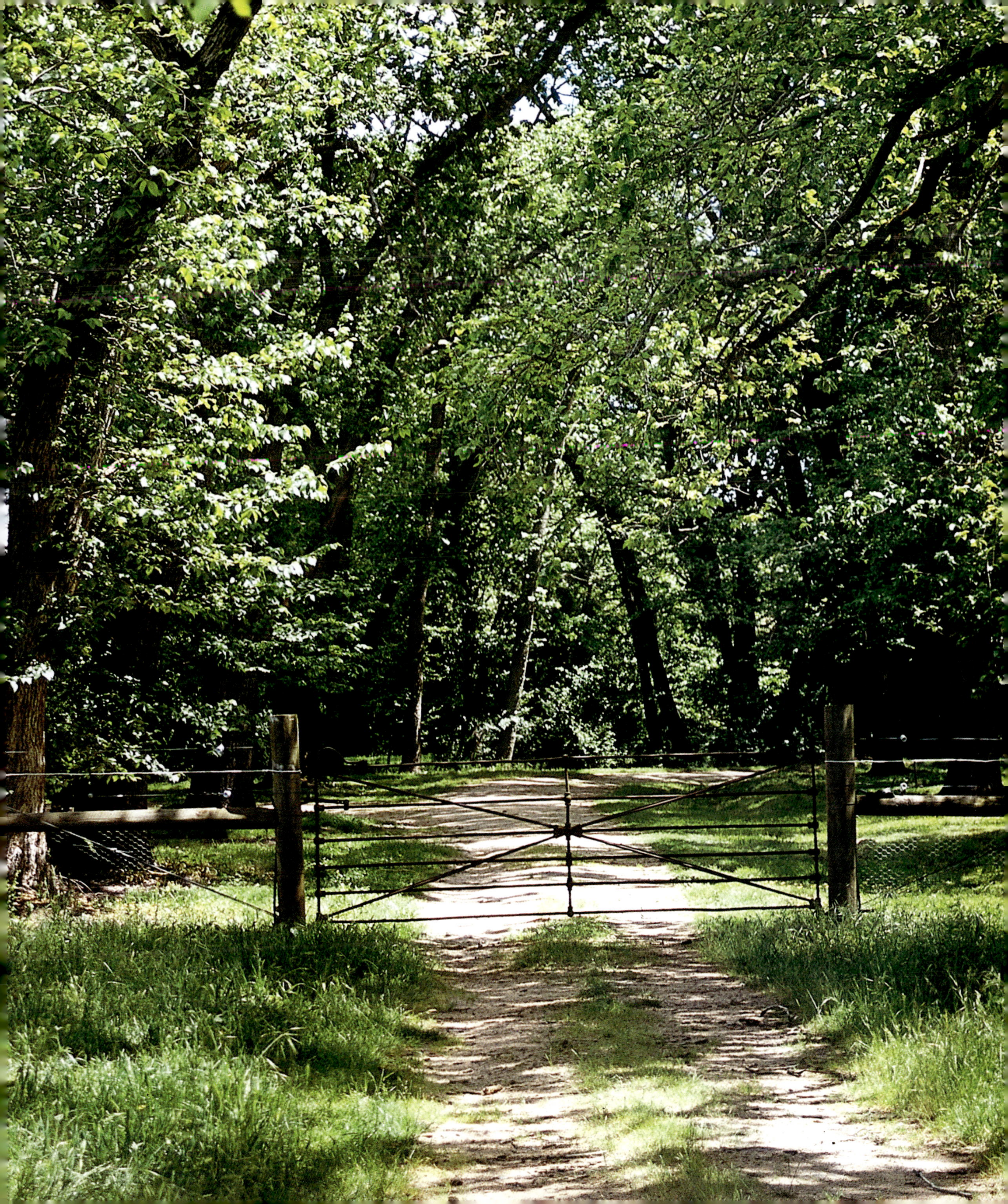

Ercildoune has had a history as magnificent as its architecture. The property was purchased by Sir Samuel Wilson, a man who had made his fortune from linen manufacture in Ireland, and mining in Ballarat and Bendigo, in 1873 for 236,000 pounds. (One of Wilson's son later married Lady Sarah Churchill, aunt of Sir Winston, while a daughter married the Earl of Huntingdon.) Wilson enlarged the main house by increasing it to just under 100 squares, and then further added to the property by establishing a fish hatchery, a deer park, a small Angora goat herd and of course his famous merino sheep breeding program, which at one stage numbered 600,000 sheep – possibly more than anyone in the world. Wilson also organised for the construction of the walled garden.

In 1920, Sir Alan Currie took possession of the property, continuing the merino stud and fish hatchery and establishing a horse stud and hydro-electric scheme at the same time. Sir Currie and his wife employed 17 staff in total – 10 for the house and seven for the extensive garden.

The house has also played host, at one stage or another, to state governors, Governor Generals, many famous MPs and the Dukes of Windsor and Gloucester, who visited in 1934. It would have been, at one stage, one of the most popular places in Victoria for a house party of hunting, riding, shooting, fishing and tennis.

COUNTRY ESTATES

ERCILDOUNE

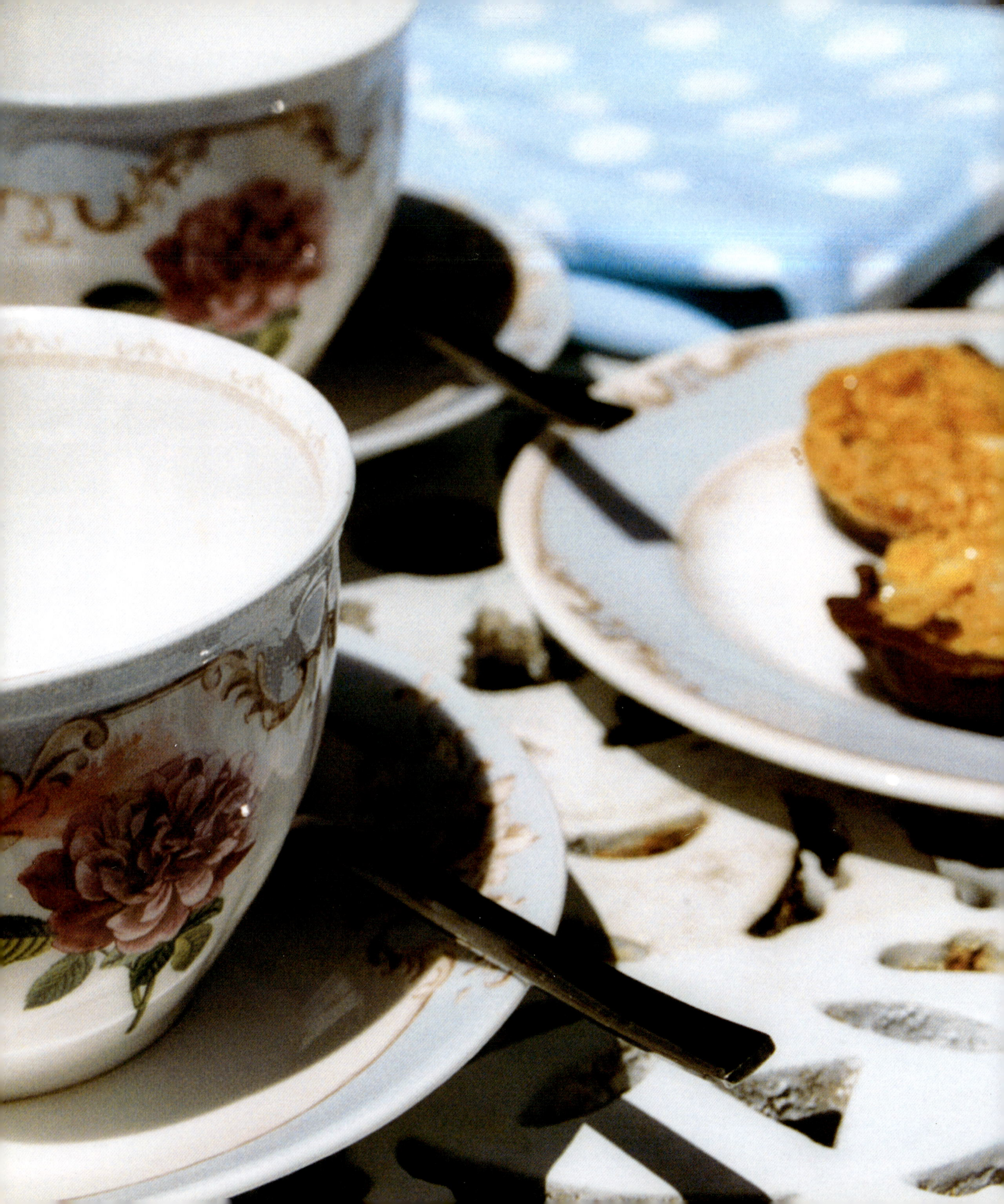

Centuries ago, many country houses were expressly for visiting. In England, the 'progresses' of Queen Elizabeth I inspired a flurry of mansion building by courtiers hoping to curry favour – many of whom bankrupted themselves in the process.

The Queen, by all accounts, was the houseguest from Hell. Sir John Puckering, in an extravagant attempt to impress her, offered Her Majesty a diamond-encrusted fan on her arrival, a bouquet containing 'a very rich jewel' between the garden gate and the house, a pair of virginals in her privy chamber and a fine gown in her bedchamber.

In addition, he was probably obliged to house and feed as many as 150 courtiers and put on wildly elaborate entertainments. Even this did not suffice, however, for the Queen, explaining that she was giving Sir John yet another opportunity to please her, pinched a salt, a spoon, and a fork, all of fair value, at the end of her stay.

ERCILDOUNE

*C*ountry life has always held a lot of cachet. For centuries the general consensus was that if you made it in the city, the first thing you did was buy a house in the country. It was the proclamation of success, of having 'arrived', if not in society then certainly in business (and very often the former followed the latter anyway).

At Hopewood, in New South Wales' Southern Highlands, there are all the signs of aristocratic ambition: a sweeping circular carriageway created around a large parterre (essential for impressing the guests), a grand white 1884 residence with extensive servant's quarters, and an astonishingly beautiful formal garden that is still considered the showpiece of the Highlands.

The residence, which was built in 1884 by Ben Marshall Osborne as his family home, is a stunning sight. The house rises up from the landscape in a way that suggests its original owner wanted to indeed show that he had 'made it'.

But if the house takes a visitor's breath away, it is the garden where they get it back again. Osborne's wife was a keen gardener and created the design for the carriageway and front parterre that still forms an integral part of the larger grounds.

The second owner, who had the unfortunate name of Lebbeus Hordern, purchased the property in 1912 and immediately added to this garden by laying out the formal areas that now form the basis of this famous estate. Under Hordern, the garden came to be considered the showpiece of the area, and featured long brick pathways, a formal rose garden and a sunken fernery garden.

The third owner, Samuel Sibley, planted thousands of tulips, before selling the property in 1943 to L.O. Bailey. Bailey was the founder of the Youth Welfare Association of Australia and used Hopewood as an ophanage for 86 orphaned children. He converted the old stables into a building known as the Pavilion, and used this, as well as the main house, to accommodate these children, all of whom were no doubt thrilled to call this rambling old place their home.

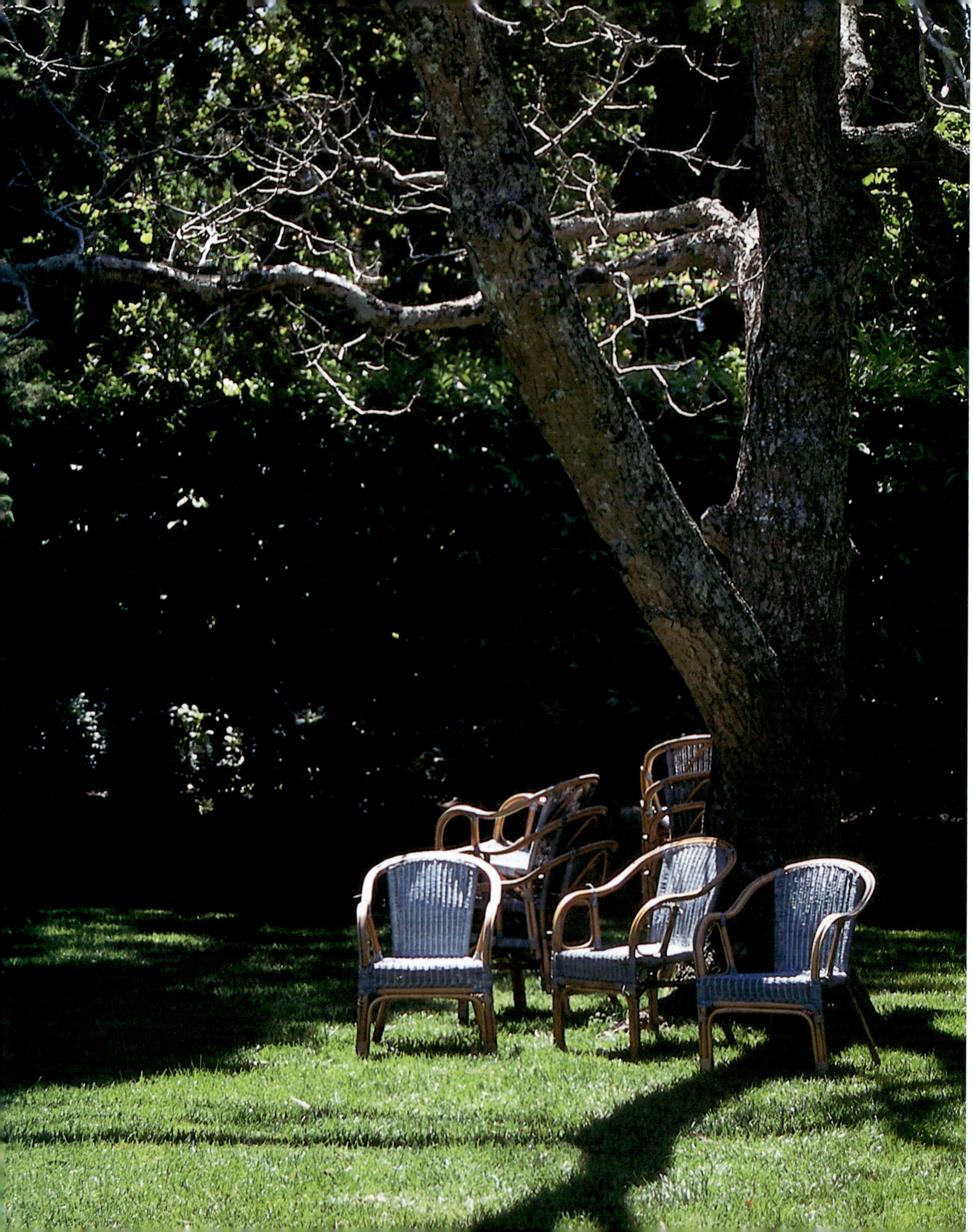

The property only passed back into private hands in 1997, when the current owners purchased it as their family home and started an extensive renovation of the house and garden, which were in a great state of neglect.

Today, while the historic homestead remains the private home of the owners, who continue to live here, the gardens have been opened to the public.

Based on the design principles of Sir Edwin Luytens the doyan of Edwardian English country garden design, the current garden's highlights include the rose pergola by the kitchen, the walled kitchen garden set in a parterre style, the woodland walk, the perennial border walk, the traditional rose garden, the reflection pond and aviary, the sunken fernery garden, the long pergola walk, the Edna Walling-inspired garden, the folly and the old ruin, which provides a stunning vantage of the cascading waterfall.

The proper name for a country estate is actually the 'seat'. The 'house' is a reference to the family lineage. Indeed, when country house purists (usually those in England – Australians generally can't be bothered with country house snobbishness) refer to the word 'house' they are referring to an urban residence rather than a rural one. The 'seat' is the ancestral home: the place when one is born, gets married, has affairs with the maid, or the gardener, in the greenhouse, runs amok in the parterre, hosts grand country house weekends, and eventually dies, usually while out shooting with one's hunting party chums. Or while one is in flagrante with the maid.

COUNTRY ESTATES

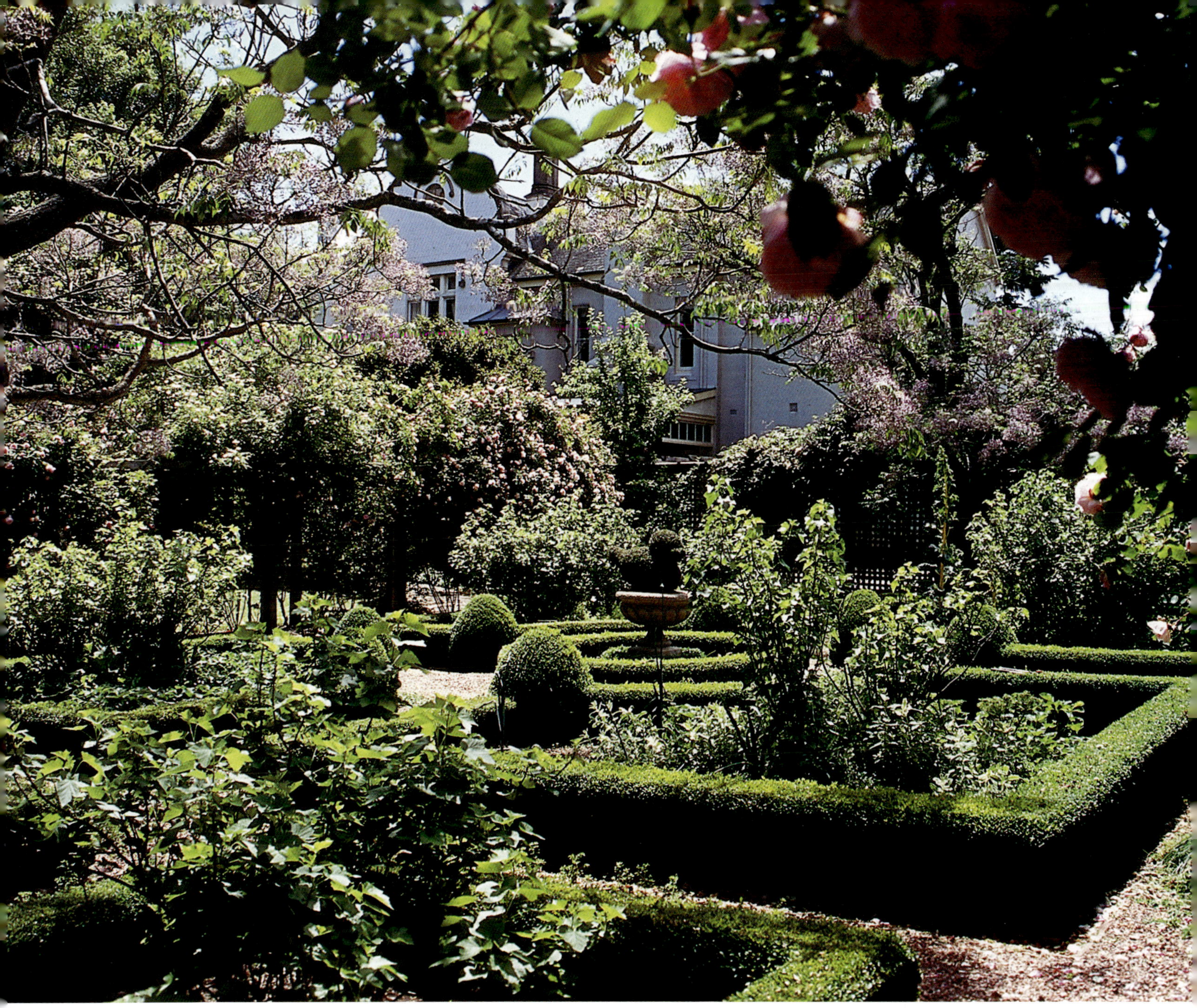

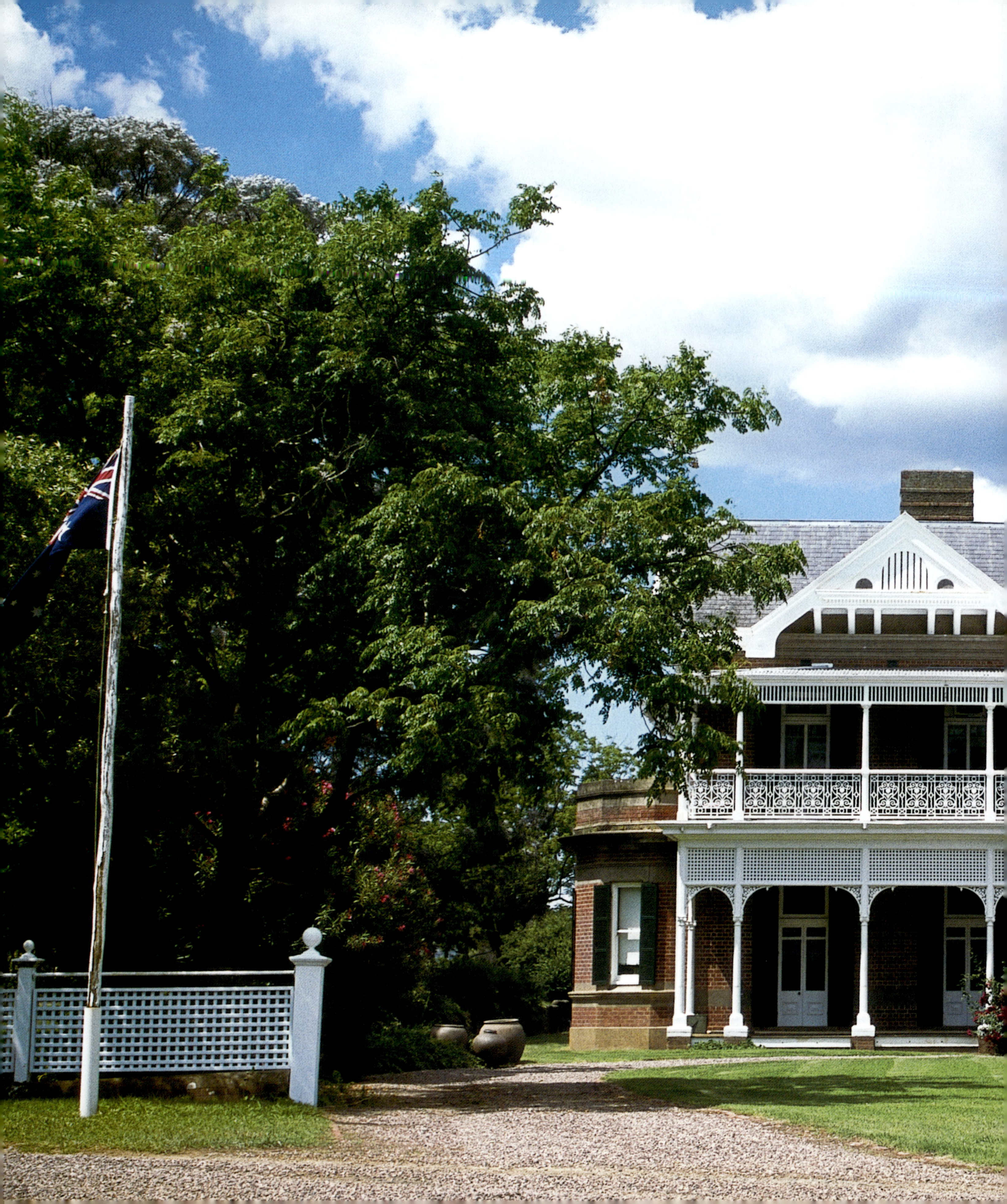

Belltrees

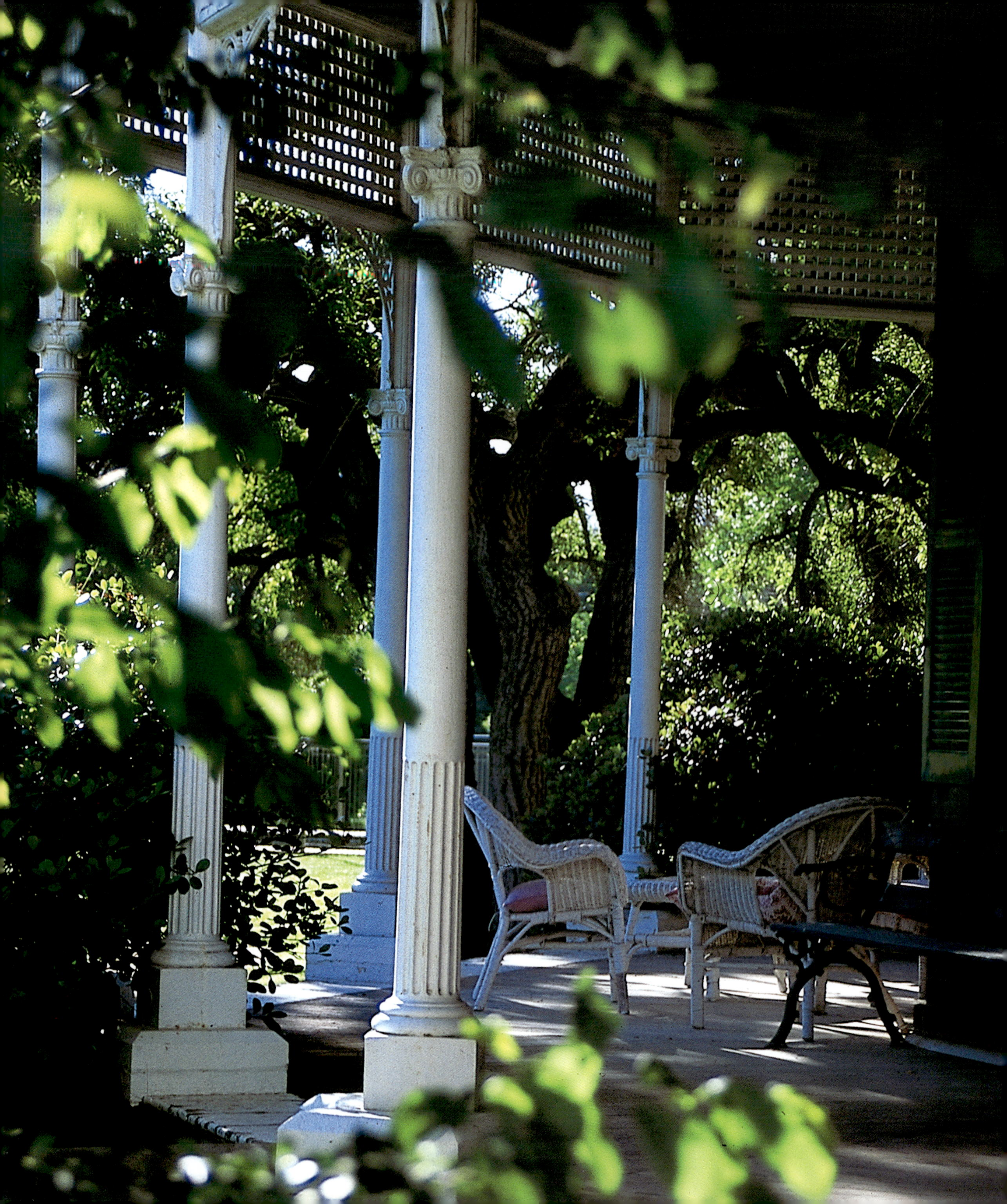

*E*ven at a glance it is easy to see that Belltrees is one of Australia's great country estates. By its original definition, a country house was the country seat of a landed family, and the centre for a vast agricultural estate that usually included – and supported – a local community, if not a small village. At the height of its power, in the early 1800s, Belltrees covered about 100,000 hectares and supported no fewer than 64 houses. The estate, which is near Scone in the Upper Hunter Valley, also had its own school, post office and chapel (all of which are still part of the estate today). It was a thriving, self-sufficient community, with the White family at the head of it all.

Now, more than 175 years later, the property has diminished in size but not in stature. The estate is only 8000 hectares now, after great tracts of land were sold off by previous generations, but the homestead is still as imposing as ever.

The 54-room, two-storey mansion is possibly one of the most beautiful Colonial-style homes in Australia, rising proudly out of the landscape like a grand old dowager that refuses to bow to modern times. The front façade, with its intricate lacework and wraparound verandah, is designed to give a sense of awe, and does just that.

Belltrees has a certain understated beauty, seen in elements like the elegant wraparound verandah where Judy White likes to read in the cool shade, and in the myriad outbuildings dotted around the property, which are almost as sophisticated as the homestead itself. Several are rented out to those who want to experience life on a grand country estate for themselves.

Inside, a lofty entrance hall, redesigned in a rich country-house red, leads to the 'rooms of parade', including a library, a billiards room, a sitting room, a formal dining room, and a vast kitchen wing with its own cooled meat room.

There are other rooms too; many, many other rooms, including one just for luggage and another just for linen. The latter is a spacious mahogany-lined space larger than most people's bedrooms with elegant ceramic markers indicating where the maids used to store each particular item – be it an eiderdown, a pillowcase, a blanket or just the bedsheets.

It is the kind of house you wish you'd grown up in, filled with fabulous secrets and curious doors at every turn, although current owner Judy White remembers hearing her husband, who grew up in the homestead, speak of being banished to the children's wing, as was customary in those days, and only allowed downstairs for the ritual summons of saying 'goodnight' each evening.

Today, Belltrees is a far different place than a century ago. Although still a formidable place to live and manage, it is efficiently run by Judy White and two of her seven children, who cleverly manage it like a corporation, organising polo and riding events, breeding cattle and polo ponies and hosting conferences, B&B stays and wedding parties.

Judy White still lives in the homestead, with her sons nearby, and mows the 2.5 hectares of lawn on her own. She also cleans the 54 rooms alone, with only the help of a half-day-a-week cleaner. It's a far cry from the days when Judy's mother-in-law first moved to the house and there was a servant behind every chair and a man hired just to clean the shoes.

Like many country houses of its type, Belltrees has 10 bedrooms, more than enough for guests – no matter how big the party. The number has come in very handy over the years: Judy White's seven children each took one as their own (and still sleep in these rooms, even as married adults). Other guests who have been more than satisfied with the accommodation include His Royal Highness Prince Charles, who slept in a single bed 'with a terrible mattress', according to Judy, but didn't complain once the entire time. Indeed, Prince Charles would often come down to breakfast singing an opera aria, so the lodgings couldn't have been too inadequate.

Belltrees has also played host to Her Royal Highness, the Crown Princess Sonja of Norway, the Govenor-General of Australia, Lord Snowdon, and the Duke and Duchess of Gloucester.

Belltrees' 52-room homestead covers 151 squares (not including the 57 squares of verandah) and includes a vast kitchen wing encompassing a large pantry, scullery, kitchen and staff quarters. There is also a nursery wing. White children were raised strictly, and rarely allowed into the formal rooms. Staff included a valet, a gardener, three cooks and a man just to clean shoes.

BELLTREES

DUCHESS OF WINDSOR BEANS

INGREDIENTS
1/2 kg of fresh green beans
1 lemon
2 tablespoons of butter

Top and tail the beans and leave whole. Undercook them. In a separate pan melt the butter and throw in the grated rind of one lemon. Remove from the heat and at the last moment toss the beans into the pan of hot rind and butter. Serve immediately. Accompany with baby potatoes and broccolini if desired.

In the library, left, Belltree's years of records are catalogued via a system of chic white volumes.

A little thank you...

Like any major undertaking, this book would not have been possible without the generous support and assistance of many people. This is a heartfelt thank you to all those who have contributed their time and effort to Country Estates.

A sincere thank you to all those country house owners who graciously let me invade their privacy and showed me around their extraordinary properties, especially Peter and Pam Habersberger at Dalvui, who not only let me visit them on a steamy hot Melbourne Cup day but generously gave me a wonderful champagne lunch at well, and Judy White, one of the most gorgeous people in Australia, who welcomed me in at 6AM on a hot summer's morning with manners that would have impressed the Queen, after I'd flown up from Melbourne and driven through the night to reach the Hunter Valley in time. Sincere thanks, too, to Chris and John Dever at Ercildoune, who also put on scrumptious pikelets for breakfast, and then proceeded to enthrall me with all the fabulous ghosts wandering around the baronial halls of this very special Scottish-inspired estate – still one of my favourite properties. Thank you, as always, to my dear friends Sally, Christine, Bruce, and Angus Schmidt at Yandina Station, which was also my home for a brief period. I do hope I can repay your generosity some day. And to Paul and Gabrielle Preat at Larundel, Jane Charlwood at Fern Vale Farm, Anne and Anthony Everingham at Mulabinba, Michelle and Michael at Cameron Lodge, Carol White at Lavandula, Paul Bangay at St Ambrose Farm, and Graham Pickles at Burrawang West Station – thank you for your help in organising shoots. It was deeply appreciated.

To those property owners who were edited from the book at the last minute due to space restrictions, my sincere apologies: you will be featured in the second *Country Estates* book, which is being worked on as I write this.

And lastly, thank you to Fiona Schultz, Martin Ford and Leigh Nankervis at New Holland publishers, who believed in this book when other publishers couldn't see the beauty of it. I want to say I told you so but I was brought up better than that.

Janelle McCulloch